Architecture for Dolls' Houses

Architecture for Dolls' Houses

Joyce Percival

GUILD OF MASTER CRAFTSMAN PUBLICATIONS LTD

First published 1996 by
Guild of Master Craftsman Publications Ltd,
166 High Street, Lewes, East Sussex BN7 1XU

© Joyce Percival 1996

ISBN 0 946819 98 X

Photography © Steve Hawkins, except Fig 4.16 © Anne Froggatt
Figs 4.28 and 6.10 © Jack Simmons
Figs 3.6–3.10, 3.12, 4.11, 4.14, 4.22, and 4.32 © Joyce Percival
Author photo © Anita Downie
Illustrations © Joyce Percival

Designed by Teresa Dearlove

Typefaces: Meridien and Helvetica
Origination in Singapore under the supervision of MRM Graphics.
Printed in Hong Kong by H & Y Printing Ltd .

To Pamela, who suggested I write this book.

Acknowledgements

I wish to thank all my friends who gave me lifts in their cars so that I could photograph various kinds of building construction in the south of England.

I also thank Anne Froggatt for Fig 4.16 and Jack Simmons for Figs 4.28 and 6.10.

The following suppliers were kind enough to send me models of construction and materials, and I thank them:

Richard Stacey, of Chichester, for models and materials shown in Figs 3.13, 4.7, 4.8, 4.12, and 4.24.

Robert Leacroft, of Kettering, for models used in Figs 8.7, 8.8 and 8.17.

Reuben Barrows, of Ilford, for material used in Figs 4.5, 4.6 and 4.26.

'Tops Houses', of Birmingham, for material used in Fig 4.36.

I also thank Peter Alden of 'Dolls' House Holidays' in Stafford for his help and advice.

Measurements

Although care has been taken to ensure that metric measurements are true and accurate, they are only conversions from imperial. Instances will be found where a metric measurement has fractionally varying imperial equivalents (or vice versa), usually within 0.1mm either way. This is because, in each particular case, the closest metric equivalent has been given, rounding up or down to the nearest 0.1mm.

Annotations to the diagrams list only imperial measurements: please refer to conversions in the text, or to the metric conversion table on page 140.

Reference sources

In addition to the many excellent books available, museums, particularly open-air museums, provide a useful and interesting source of information. Check with local Tourist Boards for locations and opening times.

Suppliers

To locate stockists and suppliers of materials referred to in this book, please consult your local telephone directory or the many magazines available. Dolls' house and miniature fairs, listed in magazines, are also helpful in locating suppliers.

Contents

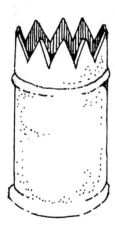

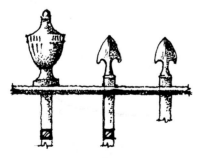

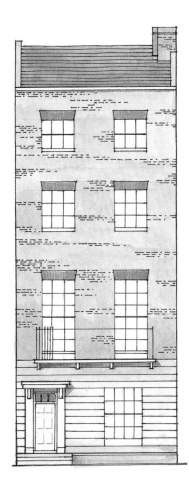

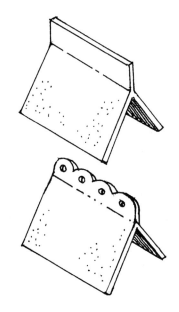

Introduction

T his book has been written for those of you who are thinking of buying or building a dolls' house and for those who already own one and who would like to achieve the 'right' feeling for your building. It has been written to encourage you to look at actual full-size buildings and enjoy relating your findings to the miniature worlds you wish to create.

I have concentrated on the external appearance of houses in England, because there is such a variety of styles and materials from which to choose, and I have chosen to focus on small to medium-sized houses because those which are larger and more complicated in plan do not readily lend themselves to 1/12, or even 1/24 scale interpretation. These scales are the ones that are most widely used at this time. Also, a large model house can be rather unwieldy, and can appear overwhelming in some domestic situations.

Many 1/12 scale, and to a lesser extent 1/24 scale, building materials and furnishings are readily available from commercial sources, but it is not necessarily difficult to achieve various effects using your own painting and modelling skills. Many of the construction ideas in this book have developed from my own thoughts and observations, and in some cases, these are illustrated with models that I have made. There are, of course, many different ways of doing things, and personal ideas and practical applications will enhance your interest and work in the miniature world. So, think about your own talents and hobbies and how they can be absorbed and developed into the work on your dolls' house to help you really enjoy yourself.

Chapter 1 Choosing a dolls' house

Whatever inspired you to enter the world of dolls' houses – perhaps you read a magazine or have friends who are enthusiastic – it is an intriguing hobby. Those who have already acquired a house will have slightly different requirements form those who are at the very beginning of this hobby, but I think that most people will find something of interest in this chapter.

Period or type

It is a good idea to read magazines and to visit shops and fairs whether you are just beginning, or looking for finishing touches. You may already have a favourite historical period in mind, in which case you could make a list of things you would like to acquire and ideas you would like to develop. If you are actually looking for a house to buy, you could go with an open mind and see what appeals to you. (I use the word 'house' in its widest sense here; you might be thinking of a shop or some other building and the same remarks apply.) Of course, you might still visit a shop or fair with a list of your requirements and then be absolutely taken aback by the various houses and furnishings on display that you never dreamed could be available. This is why it is best to come away with as much information as possible, including catalogues and addresses, and then to think hard about how your ideas and the availability of items fit together.

I must admit that this is a counsel of perfection – if you see a house and it strikes a chord, you will probably buy it and thoroughly enjoy furnishing and decorating it. However, there is one basic point that you really have to bear in mind, and that is where your house will be situated. Size is important in relation to the space the building will occupy. British dolls' houses traditionally open at the front, and perhaps one or both sides as well, so one of these can stand against a wall, but if you wish to acquire a dolls' house from the USA, you will find that it probably has an opening back, so you will need to consider its display accordingly. Whatever house you have, you will need to decide whether to leave the sides blank, as with a terrace house, or whether to continue the decoration round the sides.

Construction methods

While you are still looking for your house, the question as to whether you buy a ready-built house or one in kit form might arise, or you may consider building one to your own, or a published commercial design. Considering the first two options, there are points for and against on either side. A kit will be cheaper than the same model ready-built, but you will need to enjoy putting things together, and to have an extra pair of friendly hands available! It is easier, with a kit, to add chimney breasts and to cut cornices, dealing with a wall at a time which can lie flat on your work table. Staircase walls are easier to paper or paint before the staircase is put in, although some otherwise ready-built houses now leave the staircase loose, and it is as well to check this point if you are considering buying one. On the other hand, if you are eager to make a start actually decorating and do not wish to spend time putting the house together, then a ready-built one would be right for you: much depends on your ways of thinking and what you like doing.

If you want to build your own house right from the start, there are many books available which give detailed instructions on how to do this and Chapter 2 in this book gives a few hints on some unusual aspects of construction, and basic points to consider.

If you have little experience in this field, but enjoy making things, remember that single-storey, two-roomed rural cottages, or two-up, two-down town dwellings can be very interesting and relatively simple to make. Chapter 10 gives information about cottages which can be adapted to simple plan forms, and illustrates this with a two-room country cottage which I built to my own design.

Before you make the final decision on what to buy or build, or in what style or period to furnish your house, make sure that internal furniture and fittings are readily available at a price you wish to pay. The range of ready-made goods is very wide, from craftsman-built to mass-produced, and the quality and prices naturally vary. If your hobby is making miniature furniture, then the house will form a background for your expertise. Likewise for other hobbies including embroidery, painting and decorating.

The residents

Who is going to live in your house? Model tradespeople will not need as many rooms as those who do a lot of entertaining in a social sphere. What sort of rooms do you want to furnish? Perhaps you want a very realistic period house with period people through which an interest in furniture and costume could be indulged, or you could have a modern family living in a Georgian or Victorian house. This would give scope for a modern kitchen in a converted and restored house, as many people have today. If you choose to have an Edwardian family living in a Georgian house, that family could have retained the beautiful fireplaces of the Georgian period, and have collected Victorian furniture, and perhaps exotic items brought from overseas as was the fashion in the 1870s and 1880s.

Adaptations

You need to think about the potential of the house you see in a shop or fair for being developed in the style or period you want. For example, roofs can vary in pitch from one area of the country to another, and in different periods. You might need to do some adapting if your choice falls short on one of these. You could relate your dolls' house to a region which you know and love; perhaps you have visited it on holiday or it is within the scope of a day's outing or even within your own immediate surroundings, whether they be in the town or the countryside.

Wherever you are and wherever you visit, do look at interesting buildings and note their appearance. There are hints on how to record buildings in a simple way in Chapter 12. Knowing that this information might eventually be used in your dolls' house activities could add to your perception of your surroundings and give you an added interest in them.

Chapter 2 Dolls' house construction

There are many books and articles available which describe the basic method of building a complete dolls' house, but the aspects emphasized here are the choice of materials from which to build the carcass or framework of your house, and the modification of kits. Either birch-faced plywood or medium density fibreboard (MDF), or a combination of the two, can be used: there are advantages and disadvantages with both. It is easier to screw fixings into plywood than it is into MDF, but when paint is applied, MDF will not warp whereas plywood will, unless both sides are painted. A house built mainly of MDF will be much heavier than one built of plywood: it is worthwhile thinking about the ease – or otherwise – of moving your house about, and whether you envisage it staying in one place.

Openings

Consider how you wish your dolls' house to be viewed. It is quite usual to open the front only, and in a terrace house this is the only option, although the roof can also be made to lift off. If you have enough room, it could open on one or two sides as well as on the front. You could then plan a house two rooms deep. However, for the purposes of this Chapter, we will choose the option of a house one room deep, with its back against a wall, and only the front to open.

There are two ways of opening the front; one is to hang it on hinges, and the other is to lift it out. If you choose to hinge the front, take care that it does not swing out so far as to pull the house over. To avoid this happening, if the house is double-fronted or long and low, the front is usually hinged both left and right. This can cause an unsightly join in the front unless it coincides with a projection such as a full-height bay window. The lift-off construction does not give this problem, and has the added advantage that the front can be placed alongside the house itself, so that both can be viewed at the same time. If the front is made to lift off, you will need to fix a horizontal piece of wood to it at the base to stop it from falling over. This can be treated as a pavement or

Right **Fig 2.1 Construction of a thickened lift-off front.**

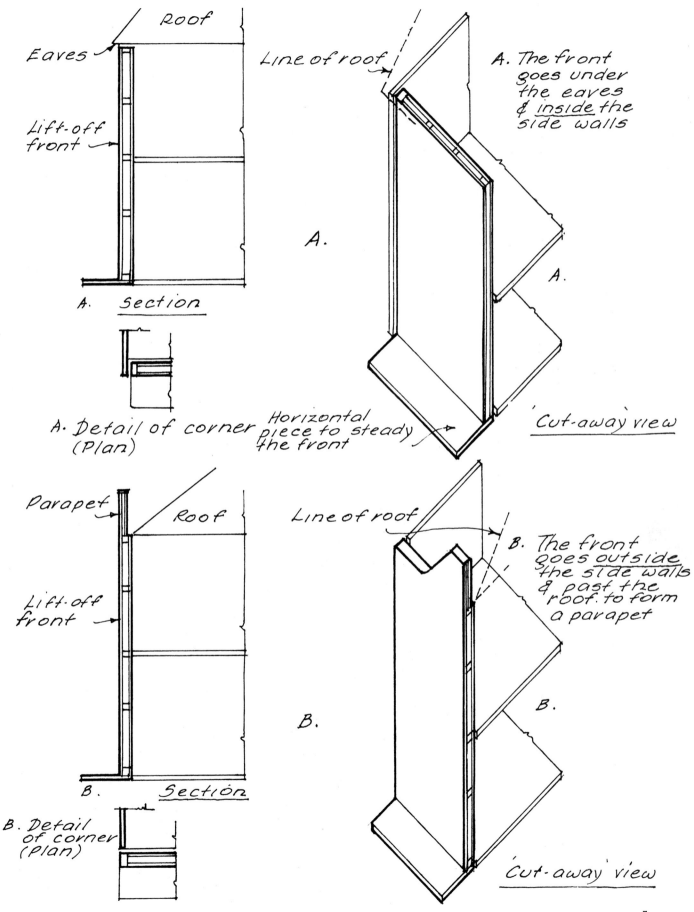

Roof

Eaves

Lift-off front

A. Section

A. Detail of corner (Plan)

Line of roof

A. The front goes under the eaves & <u>inside</u> the side walls

A.

A.

Horizontal piece to steady the front

'Cut-away' view

Parapet

Roof

Lift-off front

B. Section

B. Detail of corner (Plan)

Line of roof

B. The front goes <u>outside</u> the side walls & past the roof to form a parapet

B.

B.

'Cut-away' view

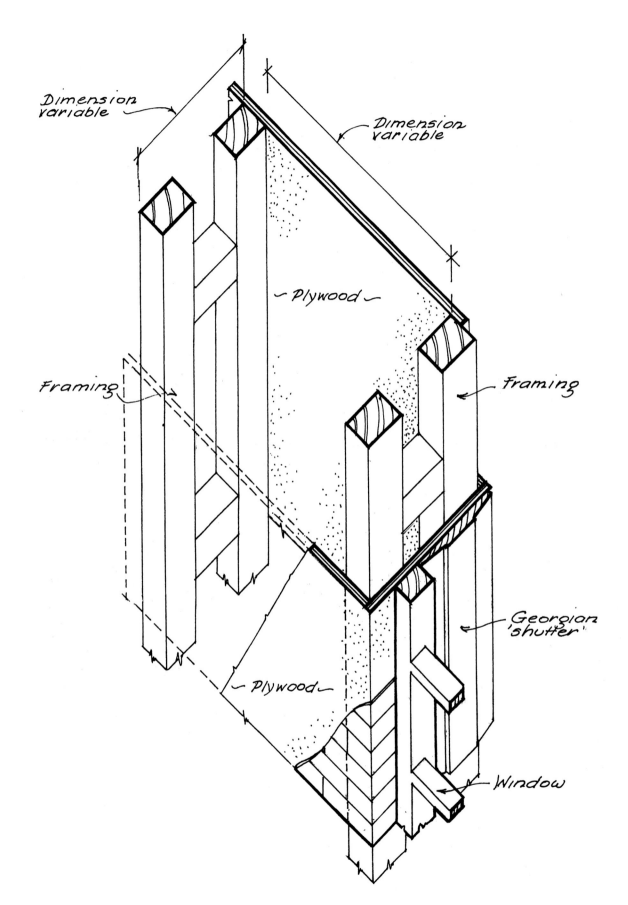

Dimension variable

Dimension variable

~ Plywood ~

Framing

Framing

~ Plywood ~

Georgian 'shutter'

Window

ornamental pathway. If the roof has overhanging eaves, care must be taken to ensure that enough room is left for the front to fit under it; this applies whether it is hinged or made to lift off. (*See* Fig 2.1.)

Consideration should be given to methods of finishing the back of the opening front. The windows will be curtained to match the rooms behind, because these will show when the front is closed, but you might wonder whether it is necessary to paint or paper the walls to match those inside – it is if you propose to hang mirrors on the back walls, because they will reflect the finish when you look through the windows, especially if the house is lit, but otherwise, it is enough to paint or paper the rear of the hinged or lift-off front in a pleasant toning colour.

Following on from the mention of lighting, make sure that your lighting fittings will run on a suitable circuit, uninterrupted by opening parts of the house. The various lighting systems that are available will give details of the points to be considered.

Windows and walls

Still working on the main carcass of the house, think whether you would like the windows to appear set in a thick wall. Such thick walls are particularly noticeable in slate-built cottages in the Lake District and in cob-built cottages in the south-west of England. When windows are set back in a dolls' house, they give a realistic depth to the walls. Most houses and kits bought from commercial sources use ¼in (5mm) plywood or MDF which is not thick enough to set windows in, or to allow for the insertion of the wooden folding shutters which were such a feature of some Georgian houses. Thickening of the external walls of your dolls' house can be

Left **Fig 2.2** Thickening external walls.

Below **Fig 2.3** Thickened walls to take set-back windows.

Below right **Fig 2.4** A thickened wall makes a deep window sill possible.

carried out quite easily, however, by adding an internal leaf of thin plywood, as shown in Figs 2.2, 2.3 and 2.4. These show a wall thickened to take Georgian shutters; the wall can be made any thickness, but if you are adapting a kit, any reduction in the size of the rooms should be considered. The sizes and numbers of the wooden pieces used in making the framework will depend on the required thickness of the wall and its height; smaller pieces will be sufficient for a single or two-storey cottage, while a tall, Georgian or Victorian front will need substantial framing. This particular construction should be made on a lift-off front, not a hinged one, because the extra weight involved could be too heavy on the hinges. (*See* Fig 2.1.)

Internal layout

Although this book deals with external appearances, this Chapter crosses over into the interior, because it is not really practicable to separate the two when considering the construction of the whole building. The above method of thickening walls can also be applied to internal walls where houses already built, or in kit form, have doors cut in places not suitable for your proposed furniture layout. You can take a sheet of Foam-core or similar, and cut two new walls to cover the unwanted opening on both sides. You can then place a false door somewhere else in the layout, if it is necessary. (*See* the section on The Plans in Chapter 5.)

Chimneys and fireplaces

Another point to be considered, concerning an external detail reflecting an internal use, is that chimney stacks and fireplaces should connect: do not build your stacks until you have worked out the internal arrangement of fireplaces – one above the other if possible. Fireplaces were arranged one above the other for reasons of support. A fireplace flue is, essentially, a continuous hole in brick or stonework, rising through a building to gather into a chimney stack, with bends to prevent downdraught, the exception to this being Tudor fireplaces where the flues were straight. The brick or stonework needs to be quite thick. In old buildings, the weight of upper floor fireplaces had to be supported from below. As the framework of the flue from the ground floor fireplace had to be constructed anyway, fireplaces on succeeding floors used this as their support, and so, were built one above the other (*see* Fig 2.5). If your house is one of a terrace – like many Georgian town houses – then you will have projecting chimney breasts inside each room. These were a beautiful feature of many Georgian homes. Small Victorian terrace houses made much of their projecting chimney breasts in their kitchens, where cooking ranges were placed. (*See* the sections on plans in the period chapters for details on the placing of fireplaces.)

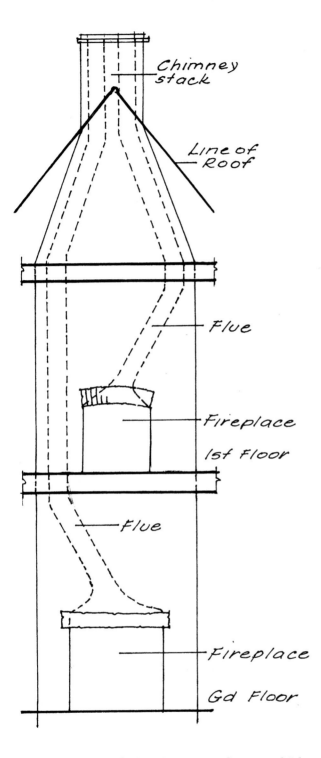

Chimney stack

Line of Roof

Flue

Fireplace 1st Floor

Flue

Fireplace Gd Floor

In Georgian and Victorian terrace houses which were more than two storeys, the arrangement of flues became more complicated. Fireplaces became smaller on the upper floors (because the rooms were less important), but the chimney breasts became wider to accommodate the flues below. Sometimes the fireplace appeared to be off-centre if it accommodated a single flue on one side and two on the other. For the purposes of a dolls' house, it is enough to place the chimney breasts centrally over one another.

Fig 2.5 Common arrangement of fireplaces and flues in buildings from the late Stuart times onwards.

Staircases

If you are building a house from the beginning and it has floors above the ground floor, design the staircase first so as to make sure that it will fit into the proposed height of your room (including the floor thickness), and the proposed length of the hall or landing. Staircases available commercially are usually set at 45° from the horizontal, so the treads and risers have the same dimensions. This is usually quite acceptable for small houses and cottages, but you might wish to have a gentler rise where the stair forms the focal point of a Georgian entrance hall. The treads, therefore, will be wider than the risers are tall, and thus the whole stair will take up more length on plan.

Roofs

One very important point to be considered regarding the appearance of a house, is the pitch or slope, and the shape of its roof. In traditional houses, the slope of the roof was related to the ability of the roofing material to throw off rainwater and snow, and to cope with the force of the prevailing wind. When constructing your roof, think about where your house is situated (*see* Chapter 3 for guidance; *see also* the sections on Roofs and Chimneys in the period chapters), and cut your material, as far as possible, in accordance with the recommended slopes. A table of pitches for roofs is given at the end of this Chapter, together with diagrams of some different kinds of roofs.

Quite a few commercially available dolls' houses are finished with the roof at an angle of 45°. This is very economical in material because two identical triangles can be cut from a square. This slope is often near enough to the ideal to give a good impression, but if you are designing and building your house from the beginning, you might wish to consider other angles which are more accurate.

Right **Fig 2.6 Various roof types.**

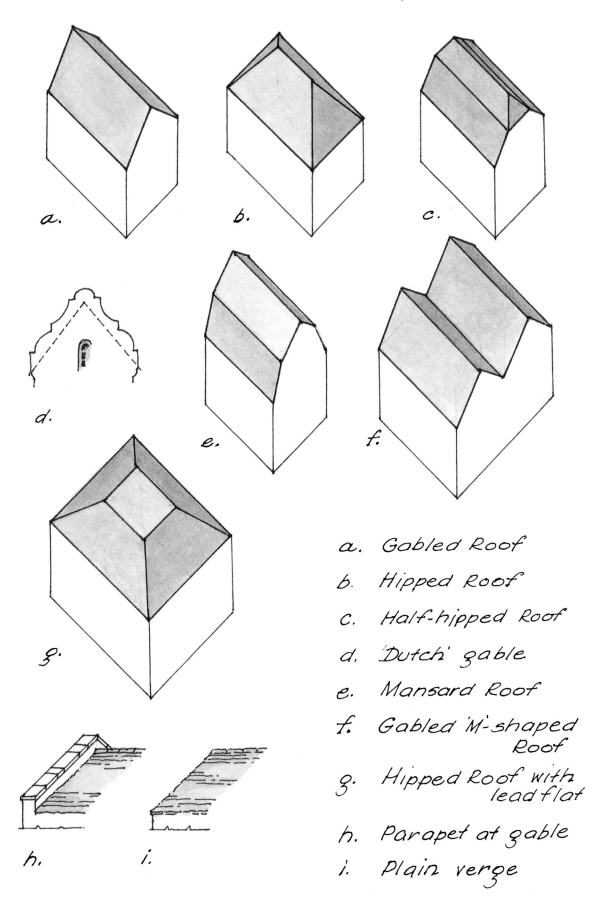

a. Gabled Roof

b. Hipped Roof

c. Half-hipped Roof

d. 'Dutch' gable

e. Mansard Roof

f. Gabled 'M'-shaped Roof

g. Hipped Roof with lead flat

h. Parapet at gable

i. Plain verge

Some general hints on construction and finishes

(*See* period chapters for specific effects.)

A	Slightly underestimate timber sizes, rather than make them clumsy.
B	Use self-hardening clay, Fimo or similar to create artificial stone items, carved stone lintels or decorative slabs.
C	Create curved items by using the strip paper method of papier-mâché. (*See* Pantiles in Chapter 4; *see also* point C, Hints on achieving Stuart effects, in Chapter 7.)
D	To imitate surface carving, stick embossed paper, lace or braid onto the item and paint it, taking care to push the paint well into the crevices. Lace and braid give a sharper appearance than embossed paper.
E	When painting any part of your house, use matt or satin-finish paints. Remember that colours which appear right on full-size buildings will need to be subdued for your dolls' house, or they will be too bright.
F	If you are staining wood, remember that the grain will be emphasised by doing so; choose close-grained wood and wood that has been specially selected for dolls' house work, to avoid the grain looking out of scale.
G	Try to give your buildings a weathered look. Dab the base of external walls with a little light grey or brown paint, and blend it with the wall finish. Smear a little paint or use crayon on the walls below the ends of windowsills. Weather old roofs of limestone slabs or clay tiles by dabbing on matt enamel in a few places – greens for moss or orange for lichens. Look at old buildings to see where the stains are, and go lightly with the paint or crayon.
H	Acrylic paste is useful for imitating semi-smooth or rough surfaces, such as stone walls or roofing slabs. Chapter 4 gives suggestions for where it can be used. It can be obtained through artists' suppliers, as it was originally developed for artists to achieve textured effects in their work. Many different textures are available from different manufacturers, and some can be used straight from the jar while others need water or glue added. Plywood varies in quality and can be very absorbent, so when using the paste on a plywood base, the plywood should be given a thin coat of acrylic primer to prevent undue absorption of moisture from the paste.

I

Tetrion or Polyfilla can also be used to imitate stonework. Both are used in their powdered form and mixed to a paste with water. However, to reduce the possibility of the mix coming away from the plywood or MDF backing, it is advisable to introduce some PVA glue in some way – recommendations for methods of doing this vary. Here are two which I have not actually tried myself, but which have been given by two practising dolls' house builders. For both of these methods, the paste should be laid about 1/16in (1.5mm) thick. They are as follows:

Method A

Dilute PVA glue with 50% water, and mix with the powder to make a modelling consistency. (Only experimentation will enable you to judge this.)

Method B

Apply a coat of PVA glue, diluted with two parts of water (sizing), to the basic structure. Mix the powder with water, to give a modelling consistency, and apply immediately to the sized surface. You might need to apply the sizing and paste in small areas so that they don't dry too quickly for you to carry out the modelling work.

Pitches of roofs for different materials

Thatch
Not less than 45°

Pantiles
30 to 45°
Sometimes you will see pantiles laid to a much steeper slope than the 30° recommended minimum; this is often because they are being laid on the timbers of a previously thatched roof, the thatch having fallen into disrepair. A pantiled roof was much lighter than one covered in plain tiles, so the timbers of a previously thatched roof could take the weight.

Ordinary plain clay tiles
45 to 55°
If the gable is narrow, as with some Victorian roofs, the pitch can be increased to 60° if it improves the appearance.

Stone slabs
25 to 35°: 47 to 60°
The pitch depends on the weight of the slabs. Heavy ones, such as those used in the Pennines, have a slope of 25 to 35°. Lighter ones such as those found in the Cotswolds, were given a pitch from 47 to 60°, a common one being 55°.

True slates from the Lake District, Cornwall and Wales
Minimum pitch 25 to 30°
The Welsh slates widely used in the late Victorian period were laid to much steeper pitches than this in some detached villas, where the design required it.

Lead
It is worth noting that 'flat' roofs were laid to a slight fall to facilitate drainage
This was used to cover flat and low-pitched roofs from Georgian times onward. Lead was also used for covering curved surfaces such as turrets, domes and roof lanterns through the ages. The lead sheets were laid on an underlying timber structure.

Chapter 3 Influence of local materials

An awareness of the many colours and textures that exist in buildings throughout England will enable you to incorporate some of them into your dolls' houses to give them a unique and authentic appearance.

The names of counties are no respectors of the natural disposition of materials used in old buildings, so, where the name of a county is given, it is only indicative of the general area under consideration. Also, some materials from Wales and Scotland were used in English-built houses when improved transport made them more widely available.

Variety

Materials used in old buildings were derived from the underlying geological structure of the country, and this was the principal physical factor in determining regional styles. Because the geological formation of the British Isles is so varied, throughout its length and breadth, it follows that the stones and clays quarried and dug from it through the centuries possessed many different characteristics. The thickness of overlying soil, together with local climatic conditions, also influenced the disposition of old forests which yielded timber for building.

Colour

Varied building materials gave colour, texture and form to the villages, hamlets and towns in the countryside, and we are fortunate in being able to appreciate these still today. Looking at colour, for instance, you will find that bricks can be red, orange, brown, grey or beige-white, and the ends can be purple-blue where they have been overburnt. The colour of stone can vary from cream, through buff to yellow and brown, and on to browny-grey. Some sandstones are pink and red, and some granites are reddish-purple. There are grey-blue slates and green-blue slates; brown thatch and newly laid golden thatch; orange-red tiles and dark red tiles, even brown and purple ones. Weathered oak can be a lovely

Opposite top **Fig 3.1** A group of Cotswold buildings, built of warm golden limestone.

Opposite centre left **Fig 3.2** The cool greys of slate and granite in a Cornish fishing village.

Opposite bottom left **Fig 3.3** The warm greys of Purbeck limestone in a Dorset village.

Opposite centre right **Fig 3.4** This Kentish group displays the warm colours of tiled roofing, silver-grey weathered timbers with plastered panels, orange-red bricks, and white weatherboarding.

Opposite bottom right **Fig 3.5** A Sussex street with houses built from weathered timbers and plastered panels. Roofs vary between Horsham stone slabs and clay tiles.

silver-grey. All these colour variations are wonderful and provide great interest. Figures 3.1–3.5, 3.11, 3.14 and 3.15 show the range of colours and building styles in some of the villages across England.

Colour can change under different lighting and weather conditions, so when you are looking at a particular building material, think of the conditions that are present at the time. For instance, honey-coloured Cotswold stone is enhanced under a soft sun, which makes the colour glow. Granite and slate can look uninteresting in sunlight, but their colours can be brought up with a shower of rain, much as beach pebbles look brighter under water. Portland stone bleaches to an eye-blinding white under strong sunlight, while red brickwork looks warmer under a soft evening sun. Note the aspect of colour you prefer, and try to match it in your dolls' house.

Transport

From early times up to the early nineteenth century, small houses were built from the materials which were locally available. This was because transport was very difficult along the rutted, unmade roads of those early times. When roads became better in some – but not all – areas, and canals were an economic proposition, building materials were easier to transport to distant places. With the coming of the railways, there was a large increase in the transport of materials. Sometimes, in the case of bricks, it was easier to import them from a brick-earth area than to quarry local stone. So, in some places, nineteenth-century brick buildings became mixed in with older, mellow, stone ones.

Building materials

Up to the nineteenth century, the very small, humble peasants' dwelling was either built of timber, the cheapest material ready to hand and the most easily worked by the unskilled workman, or, in stone districts, it was built of undressed stones placed one on top of another. In some remote areas of Britain, the walls were constructed of turves. Roofs of these little dwellings were made from turf or heather.

Larger houses dating from the late Middle Ages, and occupied by such people as yeoman farmers, merchants and tradespeople, were built quite substantially. Very large houses, belonging to those whom we would call the aristocracy, were often built of stone or brick, even if this had to be brought from a distance.

When you travel through different parts of England, you will soon see the differences between one area and another, between those of stone, slate, timber, brick and flint and many other materials, some very localized. Figures 3.6–3.10 show details of some of the building materials and methods found in the south-east of England.

Stone

Stone buildings alone show many different characteristics depending on their location. Old stone houses in the Cotswolds have thin stone slabs on the roofs while stone houses in Cornwall, because of the local slate there, have slate roofs. The stone houses of the Lake District have slate roofs for the same reason, but the slate is quite different in appearance from Cornish slate. Although they are all built of stone, these buildings look different. This is because the stone of the Cotswolds is what a builder would call soft limestone, which can be easily worked to form mouldings and decorations, whereas the stone of Cornwall includes granite which is very hard to work, so the buildings have a stern appearance. The houses of the Lake District have walls built from thick slabs of greenish, bluish purple slate, the blocks of which were laid with very little binding material between the slates, and sloping towards the outside of external walls.

The northern counties of Yorkshire, Derbyshire and Lancashire show particularly striking differences in their building stones; the dark sandstone walls of the uplands contrast vividly with the light limestones of the Dales. Roofs in these areas are usually heavy stone slabs of a brownish colour, although houses on the Yorkshire coast are usually roofed with red or brown pantiles.

A narrow part of the Midland area is formed from the limestone belt which stretches from Dorset in the south to Yorkshire in the north, and yields a particularly fine quality building stone which is capable of being very finely carved. Sandstones cannot be so finely detailed.

Limestones of the south, south-west and west vary in colour from dark cream to soft brown. Cotswold stone is an overall golden yellow, though it varies throughout the area, for example, stone found in Broadway is darker than that found in Chipping Campden. Houses are either roofed with matching stone slabs, graded from large at the eaves to small at the ridge, or, in some outlying villages, are thatched.

The most important building limestone of Dorset is Portland stone. This is well known for its use in seventeenth-century London after the Great Fire. Christopher Wren built St. Paul's Cathedral from stone from the Isle of Portland and used it in conjunction with red brick in the seventeenth-century part of Hampton Court Palace. It bleaches to a bright white and can be very obtrusive in unsuitable surroundings. On the Isle of Portland, which itself is a giant block of limestone, the buildings all blend one with the other. The other building stone of Dorset comes from the Purbeck Hills, and the village houses built of this are either roofed with slabs of the same stone, or are thatched.

Kent, which is mainly a brick and timber area, has some stone available from the greensand, which is used in simply dressed blocks, especially in church walls. There is also a form of sandy

Opposite top left **Fig 3.6**
A small house, one of a terrace, with a clay-tiled roof, clay tiles hung on the upper floor, and the lower one built of Kentish ragstone, with brick corners.

Opposite bottom **Fig 3.7**
Part of an eighteenth-century church wall in Kent. The golden-yellow stone is Wealden sandstone, and the grey blocks are from the greensand.

Opposite top right **Fig 3.8**
Corner of a Kentish building showing brick and flint, stained weatherboarding, and mathematical tiles which look like brick, though the junction with the weatherboarding shows that they are not what they seem.

limestone, called Kentish Rag, which is difficult to work into rectangular blocks, but splits naturally into various polygonal shapes. A dark golden-brown sandstone from the Weald was used in some churches, for example Mereworth, and in some large houses for the aristocracy.

Timber

The counties of Kent and adjoining Sussex have an abundance of half-timbered houses where the oak framing has weathered to a silver-grey colour. The spaces between were filled with panels made from hazel or willow wands (long, slender, pliable shoots), which were plastered, and the whole was known as wattle and daub filling. These were then lime-washed white or cream.

In districts where building stone was not readily available, you will find a lot of these timber-framed and plaster finished houses, although they differ in character according to where they are situated. In East Anglia, for example, plaster could cover all of the framing, or, alternatively, the spaces between. The plaster was

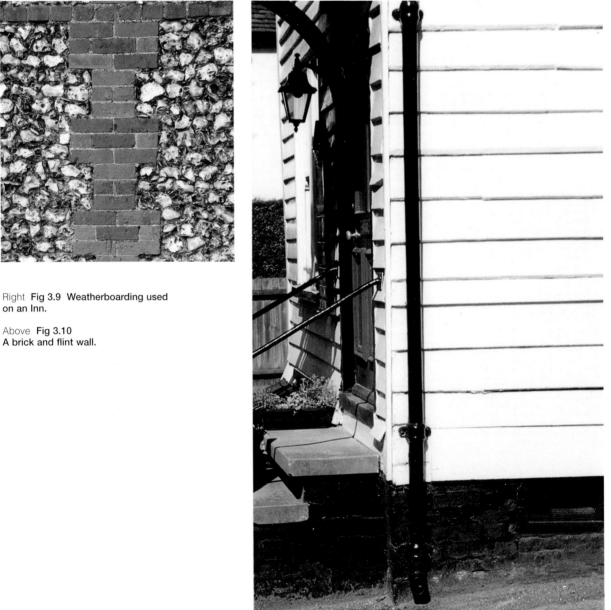

Right **Fig 3.9** Weatherboarding used on an Inn.

Above **Fig 3.10**
A brick and flint wall.

Fig 3.11 This cottage, from the Hereford-Worcester district, shows the heavier timbers of the area, which were blackened by the Victorians.

limewashed and sometimes left a natural colour, but quite often was coloured with natural earth colours and other pigments to give the characteristically local colours of cream, yellow, buff, orange and Suffolk pink. The latter was made by adding bulls' blood to the basic limewash mix, originally giving a deep red colour which rapidly faded to a warm pink. (This colour is now produced artificially!)

In the Worcester and Hereford region and adjoining areas, the principal walling materials are seen in brick, timber, limestone and sandstone. The sandstones are overlaid with clays which, in the past, gave rise to the growth of dense oakwoods. The forests in this part of England were cleared later than in other districts, so the tradition of building in timber persisted until a comparatively late date. The characteristics of West Midland half-timber buildings arise from the use of very heavy timber frames, and square or oblong plastered infill panels. In important town buildings and gatehouses, decorative timber infill pieces were also incorporated. These buildings have quite a different character from those in the south, south-east and east of England. In these latter areas, in certain places where iron ore was dug, the oakwoods were exploited for charcoal burning in Tudor times, and there was some anxiety that timber might be in short supply for the building of large ships, so the use of timber for purely decorative purposes was kept to a minimum.

When softwood was imported at the end of the eighteenth century and through the nineteenth century, a form of timber cladding, known as weather-boarding, became popular in the south-east and east of England. (*See* Timber, under Walls in Chapter 8.)

Brick

You will find brick buildings where there is an abundance of brick earths and the main brick earth areas include Kent, Sussex and Surrey, most of the London area, part of East Anglia, and up towards Peterborough. There is also brick to be found in Gloucestershire around Tewkesbury, and near Worcester. In the otherwise predominantly stone region of Dorset, there is also a band of brick earths. The town of Blandford was rebuilt in brick after a fire in the early eighteenth century. Bricks were made by digging the clay – which was earth that had become compressed – forming it into bricks by hand, and burning these. In some areas, the same material was also used to form tiles for roofs, or for hanging as a wall covering on a timber frame behind. (This is a notable feature of houses in Kent, Sussex and Surrey). London possesses an abundant supply of brick earth in the Thames Valley, and many of the Georgian buildings of London were built from this.

Brick was also used from the end of the seventeenth century in the infill panels of half-timber houses and cottages, where the earlier wattle and daub had decayed.

An imitation brick, known as a mathematical tile, was popular in the south of England in the eighteenth century and onwards. It was made from brick earths and hung vertically on timber framing. The finished flush surface was indistinguishable from genuine brick. Its main purpose was to provide a cheap alternative to ordinary bricks, while looking like the real thing. (I include this reference as a matter of interest only, because the dolls' house builder will probably concentrate on ordinary brickwork.)

In the early nineteenth century, many brick buildings in towns and cities were covered in stucco. This was made from a form of coloured cement, mixed with water to form a thin paste, and applied to brickwork. Some people thought that stucco, which was supposed to imitate stone, gave a wealthy appearance to a building because only wealthy people could afford to build in real stone.

In the nineteenth century little back-to-back houses were run up quickly to house the influx of people from the countryside, who were flocking in to look for work in the industrial towns of the Midlands and north of England. These houses were built of cheaply produced, machine-made bricks. Wealthy people built their substantial houses of better quality machine-made bricks, many of them available in the reds, blues and purples typical of the late Victorian period.

Flint

In East Anglia there is an abundance of flints which are taken from the chalk and clay. Because there was no suitable local stone for building, flints were used. By themselves, they can only be built with rounded 'corners', and flint walls and round towers are very

Simulating flint

Packets of flints are commercially available, and can be used on their own, or with extra stone or brickwork. An example of how they can be used in a wall with brick corners is shown here in Fig 3.13.

characteristic of small churches in East Anglia. Flints were often knapped, that is, split, and the shiny faces thus revealed were used in conjunction with stone brought from other areas. They made beautiful, patterned panels which can be seen in the large churches at Long Melford, Lavenham, Southwold and Bungay among others.

In Kent, Sussex and Essex, round flints from the chalk were used, unknapped, in the walls of small houses and cottages. Rounded pebbles from the beach were used in the same way in these areas and other places in southern England. Flints are also found in the clay areas of Kent and Surrey, Oxfordshire and Buckinghamshire, where they were often roughly split and placed quite close together in the walls of buildings.

Above left **Fig 3.12** A wall of rough flint with stone corners from a church in Suffolk. The flints are local, but the stones would have been brought in.

Above **Fig 3.13** The walls for a typical East Anglian building can be simply constructed, using commercial flints and bricks.

Earth

Another walling material was earth. One of its most attractive applications can be seen in the south-west of England, where, mixed with straw and compacted, it is known as cob walling. These walls are very thick – usually a minimum of 24in (610cm) – and need to be protected from the weather. It was usual to provide a thatched roof with overhanging eaves, and to tar the base of the walls, which were built on a foundation of rubble and were limewashed white or cream. In some areas – especially in Somerset – these little houses can be seen alongside those built from roughly dressed red sandstone, locally available from the valleys in the Brendon Hills.

Below left **Fig 3.14**
Cob cottages of the south-west, with thatched roofs.

Below right **Fig 3.15**
Warm colours on plastered walls give interest to this Suffolk street.

Roofing tiles

Roofing tiles were made from the same clays as bricks, where these were still made by hand. In late Victorian times, when bricks were made by machine, buildings were usually roofed with slates, cheaply imported from the Welsh quarries. Hand-made tiles were, however, still used in conjunction with suitable bricks.

A pantile was a particular form of clay roofing tile with a shallow S-bend in section. They originated in the Low Countries (Belgium, Luxembourg and the Netherlands), and were made in such a way that fewer were needed than plain tiles to cover a roof efficiently when laid to a comparatively shallow pitch. Pantiles are found extensively in the north-east and east of England and throughout all the lowland areas adjoining the Bristol Channel. They were brought from abroad in the seventeenth century, direct to the north-eastern and eastern ports, and also to Bridgewater. From that western port, they were distributed along the Bristol Channel, and then, by way of various rivers, to parts of Wiltshire. (The word 'pantile' also describes a particular type of paving slab, some of which originally covered the historic area of Tunbridge Wells in Kent previously known as 'The Walks' and now called 'The Pantiles'.)

Thatch

To expand a little on the availability of thatched roofing, this was a particular feature of Norfolk where the reeds from the extensive water-beds of that area provided the material. Reed-thatched roofs can still be found here and in other low-lying reeded areas of England. A cheaper form of thatch was used in various country areas where it was made from the straw of wheat, barley, oats or rye, but it was not as durable as reeded thatch. Old thatch can be loose and rough while newly laid thatch appears trim and neat. Patterns made in the thatch vary throughout the southern counties and a study of these variations can be interesting.

Lead

Lead roofing was widely used on town houses and country mansions in the eighteenth century and onwards. It is a material that can be laid flat or to a very shallow slope, and the design of some sophisticated houses at that time called for shallow pitched roofs. On a steep slope, lead roofing 'creeps'. Creeping results from the expansion and contraction of sheet lead, caused by changes in temperature, and the sheets will buckle, bulge and crack if they are too large or laid incorrectly.

Because rolled lead sheets were best used in narrow widths they had to be joined together to cover the roof surface. If the roof slope was longer than the length of sheet, the next sheet would be laid to overlap it by about 3in (76mm), giving a stepped appearance to the roof.

Simulating lead roofing

Although even 'flat' roofs were laid to a slight fall, the dolls' house builder need not worry about this, as it has only a minimal effect at 1/12 scale.

The model in Fig 3.16 was made by joining the lead sheets (made from grey paper) over wooden rolls. The sheets are lapped one over the other at each roll.

Fig 3.16 Simulated lead roofing.

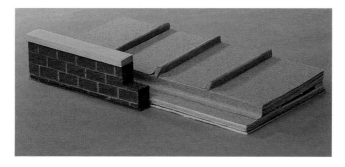

Other influences

These, broadly, were the principal materials used in the traditional buildings of England, and examples of their colour can be found in all the coloured illustrations throughout this book. The appearance of buildings was influenced not only by the materials used, but also by the way in which they were used; Chapter 4 considers some of these. Social and economic influences tended not to reach the more distant parts of the countryside until well after their absorption into the life of large towns, so simple building operations in scattered rural areas remained the same for many years. Where they were in remote places, small domestic buildings did not alter much in their external appearance between the sixteenth and eighteenth centuries.

Chapter 4 Influence of construction on pattern

I t was not only the distribution of local materials that affected the appearance of buildings, but also the use of them by local builders. The methods created the various patterns seen in English buildings, and these can be incorporated into dolls' houses.

Walls

Brickwork

Bricks have varied in size throughout the ages from 2in (51mm) thick, to just under 3in (76mm) thick. They have also varied in quality of finish, from rough in Tudor times to more precise in the Georgian and Victorian periods. While early Tudor brickwork showed an irregular bond, a more precise form of English bond was

Top left
Fig 4.1 English bond.

Top right
Fig 4.2 Flemish bond.

Bottom left
Fig 4.3 Stretcher bond.

Bottom right
Fig 4.4 Tudor brickwork.

Simulating brick

■ The dolls' house builder can buy sheets of strong, impregnated, bonded material, embossed to show Flemish or stretcher bond. The colours of these sheets, pleasant reds and greys, can be altered a little by painting with acrylic paints, which can be bought from artists' suppliers and used straight from the tube.

■ Bricks can also be individually cut from wood strip, and coloured with thin coats of matt enamel or acrylic paint. This method is useful if you wish to create a particular bonding pattern or colour, but is time-consuming for a large area!

■ It is also possible to buy brick slips which are cut from real bricks – these are available in many colours. It is not always realized that the overall colour of a brick wall owes as much to the colour of its mortar joints as it does to the colour of the bricks themselves: coloured grouts used for ceramic tiles, can be used for dolls' house mortar joints.

used from the mid-sixteenth century through to its end. Flemish bond was introduced in the seventeenth century, and was the favoured bond from that time. Stretcher bond was used for cladding walls of cheaper material or for infill panels. In the late nineteenth and twentieth centuries it was, and still is, used in cavity walling. Various patterns of brick bonds can be seen in Figs 4.1–4.4, and Figs 4.5–4.8 show how some of these can be achieved.

There are many variations of brick bond to be found, some incorporating overburnt headers (ends of bricks) as decorative features. The Victorians used polychrome (many-coloured) bricks in various bonds. (*See* the section on Walls in Chapter 9.)

Top left **Fig 4.5** A sheet of bonded material, textured to show Flemish bond.

Top right **Fig 4.6** A sheet of bonded material, textured to show stretcher bond.

Above left **Fig 4.7** Individual brick slips laid in stretcher bond.

Above right **Fig 4.8** Individual brick slips are available in many colours. They are laid here in stretcher bond.

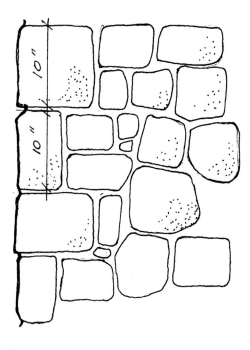

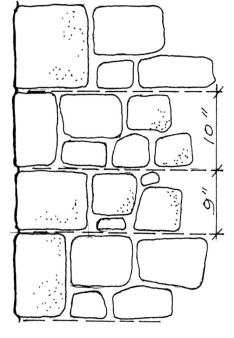

Stonework

Most types of stone can be built into walls as rubble, or can be finished finely dressed with fine mortar joints – a finish known as ashlar masonry. The term 'rubble' is given to stone roughly dressed at the quarry, which, in olden days, was at, or near, the site of the proposed building. Many variations in pattern arose from the construction of these walls. The corners of small houses and cottages were built with selected stones, carefully squared off, and in some districts, brick corners were made. Figures 4.9–4.11 show the patterns made from the construction of random rubble walls; the stones were used at random as they came from the quarry, hence the name. Mortar joints varied in width to suit the irregular stones. There

Top **Fig 4.9** Random rubble.

Above **Fig 4.10** Random rubble laid to courses which vary from 9–15in (229–381mm).

Right **Fig 4.11** Random-rubble wall laid in courses, with squared-off stones at the corner.

Rubble walls

Tetrion or Polyfilla can be used to achieve the look of rubble masonry. This method is quite complicated but gives a more regular appearance than that achieved using packets of rubble stones.

Materials

Tetrion or Polyfilla
Water
PVA glue

Method

1 Mix up powdered Tetrion or Polyfilla as described in point I, General hints on finishes in Chapter 2. (It is a good idea to make up a small amount first and apply it to a small piece of ply or MDF to a depth of about ¹⁄₁₆in (1.5mm), so that the rate of drying time and the desired consistency can be assessed before you embark on the final work.)

2 When you have assessed the drying rate – and this could be some hours – apply your mix to the wall in small areas, so that the first part does not dry out before the last is completed.

3 When your area has dried to the right consistency, take a wooden cocktail stick and mark out the joints. Take away the tiny pieces of plaster that the cocktail stick has removed and smooth the edges of each joint.

4 Leave to dry thoroughly, and then paint with matt enamel, blending different colours. Use warm greys, through to soft browns and creams for limestones; pinky reds and browns for sandstones; and cool greys, browns and pinks for granites. While the paint is still wet, sprinkle green powder (obtainable from model railway shops) at the base of the wall, to imitate moss growth. (*See* Fig 4.13.)

Simulating random rubble

For a cottage or small house built in uncoursed random rubble, the dolls' house builder can buy packets of rubble stones which can be stuck onto plywood or MDF. These can then be grouted in. (See Fig 4.12, above.) If so desired, the wall can then be painted to imitate limewash.

Above Fig 4.12 Model random-rubble wall built using commercial rubble stones.

Left Fig 4.13 A rubble wall made with Tetrion, sprinkled with green, red and yellow powder to resemble moss.

are many variations of these types of walls. In small manor houses, for example, all the stones would have been squared at the quarry to give fairly precise walling, but it would not have been as finely dressed as ashlar.

Simulating ashlar masonry

Figure 4.14 shows some old ashlar walling in a late Tudor house and Fig 4.15 shows two stages in making a similar wall, possibly of different coloured stone. To achieve the look of ashlar masonry, stick suitably sized pieces of wood or stout card onto your wall. (If you use wood, make sure that the grain follows the grain of the stone in the correct way, as it might show through the finishing coats of paint.) The joints should be very thin and filled in by smearing in grout or acrylic paste, then quickly wiping off any surplus. A simple alternative for Georgian or early Victorian buildings, where the jointing is very precise, is to paint the walls a colour suitable to represent stone and, when this is dry, paint on thin joints in a darker tone.

Above **Fig 4.14** Ashlar masonry has a smooth and regular appearance.

Left **Fig 4.15** Ashlar masonry can be made for a dolls' house, using pieces of wood or stout card.

Slate

A type of Lake District walling is shown in Fig 4.16. Buildings in that region had giant corner stones, which could measure up to 30in (760mm) deep, quarried from local stone. The main walling material was local slate, in slabs from 3in (76mm) to 6in (152mm) thick, and varying in colour through blues, greys, greens and purples. These walls were sometimes limewashed white.

Fig 4.16 This slate wall, with its giant corner stones, is typical of the Lake District.

Simulating slate

Because such a wall can vary in thickness from 24in (610mm) to 36in (910mm), or even thicker, the dolls' house builder might consider making a double wall on the front, so that a realistic thickness can be seen when looking through the windows. (*See* Windows and Walls in Chapter 2.) Samples showing how to achieve the effect of Lake District walling are shown in Figs 4.17 and 4.18. The process is rather long, although relatively simple. It involves cutting very thin pieces of balsa wood and sticking them onto your wall surface. I find that balsa wood is preferable to card, because it is easier to cut with scissors, it can split in shapes reminiscent of slates, and the grain of the wood follows the splitting planes which show up when the 1/12 scale finished surface is coloured with acrylic paint. Figure 4.17 shows the balsa on a background of unpainted plywood. Figure 4.18 shows the balsa pieces on a background of dark grey card, which emphasises the slate joints. Use Uhu glue for sticking the balsa pieces – PVA takes far too long to dry. I know that balsa and Uhu stick well on wood and card, but I have not tried it on a painted surface, so if you like the darker background, it might be as well to use card, and then stick this onto your ply or MDF walls, rather than paint the walls and stick the balsa directly onto them. Whichever you choose to do, take care not to get any glue on the surface of your masonry – paint will not take on glue.

You could, of course, do just a small part of your building in this way, and finish the remaining walls with a rough texture made by smearing a thin coat of acrylic paste over them and painting them white (*see* point H, General hints on finishes, in Chapter 2).

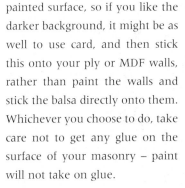

Far left **Fig 4.17** Balsa pieces stuck onto unpainted plywood to resemble Lake District slate walls.

Left **Fig 4.18** Using dark grey card to make a model slate wall will emphasize the slate joints.

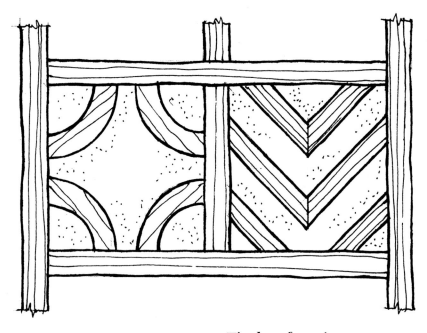

Left **Fig 4.19** Decorative patterns in timber framing.

Below **Fig 4.20** Brick-infill panels.

Timber framing

As mentioned elsewhere in this book, patterns of buildings differ depending on their location. Timber frames were generally load-bearing, but in the north-west and Midlands, additional decorative timbers were added which had no structural function. Figure 4.19 shows these purely decorative timbers set within the usual load-bearing frame. Figure 4.20 shows a load-bearing frame with brick infill panels. These usually date from the late seventeenth century onwards, and were inserted when the original plaster panels (wattle and daub) had decayed. They were laid in stretcher or herringbone bond.

The carved bargeboard was a decorative feature from Tudor times onwards and is shown in Fig 4.21. The Victorians, while using carving, also made pierced designs, which are shown in Chapter 9.

Figure 4.22 shows part of a half-timbered building with panels of decorative plasterwork, called pargetting. This was a form of decoration widely used throughout East Anglia. Sometimes, it covered the exterior of a house, the original timber frame being

Simulating brick infill

If you want to use a brick infill panel of stretcher or herringbone bond , it is as well to think of the panel dimensions before building the structural framework, so that any brick cutting is kept to a minimum. Stretcher bond is the easier of the two, and you can do away with any brick cutting by using commercial textured sheets. These can be cut with scissors or a craft knife to fit the spaces between the frames. These spaces vary between about 14in (360mm) and 27in (690mm).

Simulating carving

One way to imitate carving – anywhere, not just on bargeboards – is to stick textured wallpaper of a suitable scale and design onto the surface, and to paint it.

Left **Fig 4.21** Carved bargeboards.

Bottom left **Fig 4.22** An example of pargetting, showing incised work.

Below **Fig 4.23** Embossed wallpaper, painted to resemble pargetting.

completely hidden, as intended by the builder who had used fairly rough wood for the framing. Some of the small houses, however, had been built to show their sturdy structural timbers, (as in Fig 4.22), and had the panels between the timbers filled with simple designs. These were very attractive, and suitable for their village surroundings. In the mid- to late-seventeenth century, the art of pargetting grew into very high relief work in some wealthier merchants' properties. For the simpler designs, the village pargetter used simple wooden tools, and his undoubted skills, to produce them, pressing the tools into wet lime plaster.

Simulating pargetting

Figure 4.23 shows one simple way of achieving an effect of pargetting. Look for some embossed wallpaper and cut some suitable motifs from it. Stick the motifs in the spaces between your half-timbering, and colour them white or cream. (You could even colour them Suffolk pink, but refer to actual buildings or good colour photographs to achieve a good colour match.)

Simulating tiles

Figure 4.24 shows a model of part of a roof covered with hand-made clay tiles from the brick earth areas. This model has been made using commercial miniature tiles, stuck down singly, with the traditional overlap, onto a card base. Depending on your roof construction, this card could be plywood or MDF (*see* Chapter 2 for advantages and disadvantages of both).

The dolls' house builder can also obtain sheets of impregnated, bonded material, embossed to show tiles. These give a soft look, very effective and suitable when a more simple way of building is wanted.

Fig 4.24 Commercial tiles can be used to great effect in modelling.

Roofs

The slope and shape of roofs, and the materials used, form an important design feature of old buildings, but their effect depended also on the skill of the workers involved. Many families handed down their skills from father to son, and many of our surnames today are derived from those skills, for example, Tyler, Slater and Thatcher.

Simulating slate

Figure 4.25 shows a model of part of a roof coloured to represent grey Welsh slates: either matt finish enamel or acrylic paint can be used. This roofing is cut from sheets of moulded board, which is available commercially. It is very suitable for Victorian houses. Figure 4.26 shows part of a sheet embossed to show slates.

Above **Fig 4.25** Moulded boards can be coloured to represent slate.

Right **Fig 4.26** Sheets of bonded material are available for use in model roofs. This sheet is embossed to show slate.

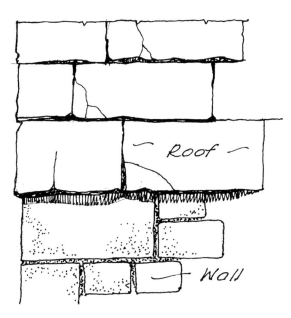

Limestone slabs

Figure 4.27 shows limestone roof slabs similar to those found in the Cotswold and Purbeck areas. Figure 4.28 shows such a roof on a church in Gloucestershire. These slabs were larger at the eaves, and were laid in diminishing courses to the ridge.

Above **Fig 4.27** Limestone roof slabs.

Left **Fig 4.28** Limestone roof slabs on a church in Gloucestershire. The slabs are laid in diminishing courses from the eaves to the ridge.

Figure 4.30 shows a model of the type of limestone slab roof found in the Purbeck area of Dorset. This roof shows a strong horizontal emphasis in the positioning of its slabs, which are pushed close together. The edges have not weathered so much as those from the Gloucestershire example.

The colour of Purbeck slabs is a warm grey, while Cotswold slabs are a dark golden-brown.

Simulating limestone slabs

■ Figure 4.29 shows how a Gloucestershire roof can be interpreted by the dolls' house builder. This sample was made from pieces of mounting card, cut to the size of the slabs – full-size slabs can measure up to 24in (610mm) long at the eaves – and stuck down to the roof surface. Acrylic paste was then spread thinly, but in an irregular fashion (maximum ¹⁄₁₆in (1.5mm) thick), over the slabs to imitate the stone surfaces, including the important edges. (*See* point H, General hints on finishes, in Chapter 2.) Alternatively, Tetrion or Polyfilla could be used. (*See* point I, General hints on finishes, in Chapter 2.) When it had completely dried, the roof was painted with artists' acrylic paint.

■ The construction of this Dorset style of roof is the same as that for limestone slabs – part has been left unfinished in Fig 4.30 to show the early stages.

■ Both samples have been partially coated with acrylic varnish to bring out the colour. Much depends on whether you want this particular effect, or you wish to achieve an old and dusty look; in the latter case, do not varnish your roof.

Above right **Fig 4.29** Model limestone roof slabs of the type found in Gloucestershire, for use in a dolls' house.

Right **Fig 4.30** A model of limestone roof slabs typical of Dorset.

Pantiles

Pantiles form a very regular, squared pattern not seen in any other traditional roofing material. They are a clay tile with a unique S-shape in section. (*See* the section on Roofs in Chapter 3.) Figure 4.32 shows part of a pantiled roof. Figure 4.33 shows pantiled roofs at Whitby. The pattern is emphasized by seagulls' droppings!

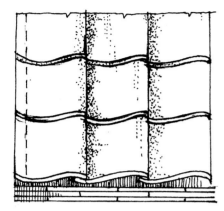

Above **Fig 4.31** The unique S-shape of pantiles.

Right **Fig 4.32** Pantiled roofs in Whitby: the bird droppings emphasize their S-shape.

Below **Fig 4.33** Method for making model pantiles.

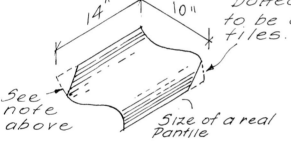

14"   10"

Dotted lines show areas to be cut away in the model tiles.

See note above

Size of a real Pantile

Cutting points for paper strips

2"

3"

Full-size section of corrugated plastic used in the model

(See text for details).

Fig: 4/12

Overlap of a real Pantile

As yet, I have not been able to find a commercial producer of 1/12 scale pantiles, but I have experimented and found a solution which appears to be quite reasonable, and which is shown in Figs 4.33 and 4.34. The latter shows a single pantile, uncoloured, and an assemblage of tiles, showing how they are put together. The method is based on strip papier-mâché work.

Pantiles

Materials

Corrugated plastic (Ideally, the tops of the corrugations should be just under 1in (25mm) apart, but those in the sample are 1¼in (32mm) apart and the effect is reasonable)

Lining paper (Obtained from a wallpaper shop)

PVA glue (Uni-Bond or similar)

Vaseline

Acrylic paint

Method

1 Cut a piece of plastic to a size easy to handle – say about 12 x 9in (300 x 230mm).

2 Cut several strips of lining paper about 11in (280mm) long, and exactly 1¼in (32mm) wide.

3 Wipe some Vaseline onto the plastic in the 9in (230mm) direction. This is to stop the first piece of paper from sticking to it.

4 Take a strip of paper and apply glue, slightly diluted, to one side, then push the unglued side into the corrugations of the plastic. Press in firmly.

5 Repeat step 4 until the sheet of plastic is full, leaving a space between each strip.

6 Take another strip of paper, apply glue to both sides, and press onto the first strip and into the corrugations.

7 Repeat step 6 until all strips of paper are covered.

8 Repeat steps 6 and 7, using about four or five strips of paper for each corrugated piece. Do not glue the top of the last strip of paper.

9 Leave the whole assembly to dry thoroughly in a dry atmosphere. Drying might take a day or two – do not hurry the process. You can prepare more strips on more plastic while you are waiting.

10 When dry, ease each strip off the plastic, and wipe the Vaseline off its base.

11 Cut carefully along each strip at the cutting points shown on Fig 4.33. You should now have several little S-shaped tiles.

12 Cut ¼in (6mm) deep by just under ¼in (6mm) deep triangular piece off each tile as shown on the diagram. (Do just a few at first to make sure one will fit into another.)

13 Now glue each tile in position on the roof. This is easier said than done, (I sometimes tried to use tiles upside down), but a look at Fig 4.34 should help.

14 When your roof is covered, paint the tiles with a reddish-brown acrylic paint, obtainable from artists' suppliers. You will need two coats. Acrylic dries relatively quickly, so it does not have time to soak the paper tiles unnecessarily.

Fig 4.34 Laying the model pantiles.

Thatch

Thatch varies in texture and pattern according to whether it is old or new, and in what part of the country it is found. Various methods of representing thatch have been described in books and magazines about dolls' house building. Results can vary quite a lot. I give here a method which I have evolved to represent rather old and rough thatch, as shown in Figs 4.35 and 4.36.

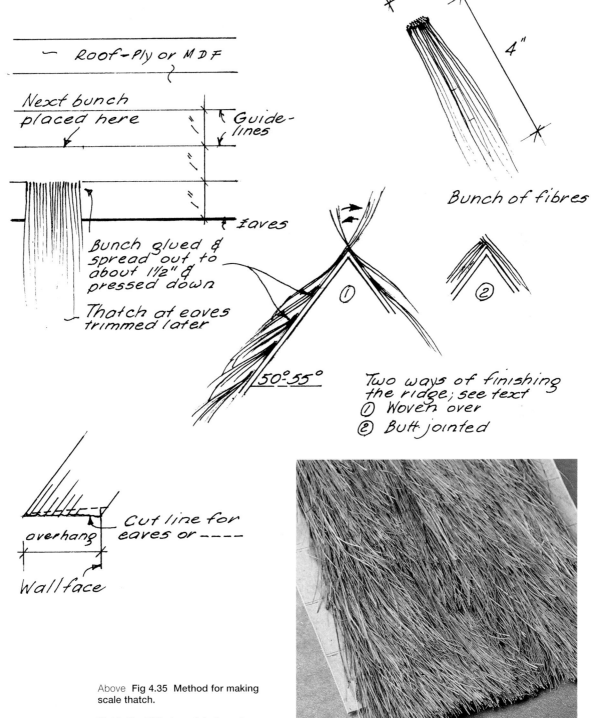

Above Fig 4.35 Method for making scale thatch.

Right Fig 4.36 A model of rough thatch.

Thatch

Materials

Bundle of coconut fibres
Uni-Bond glue or similar (put some out in an old saucer)
Plastic knife or small spatula
Scissors
Damp rags (to wipe spatula and fingers clean!)
Thin strips of balsa wood

Method

1   Draw lines 1in (25mm) apart along the roof surface, parallel to the eaves and ridge.

2   From the bundle of coconut fibres, cut off a bunch about 4in (102mm) long and ½in (13mm) in diameter. If the other end of the bunch is uneven, do not trim it; the fibres will blend more easily if they are left uneven.

3   Dip the cut end of the bunch into the Uni-Bond, to about ¼in (6mm).

4   Lay the bunch on the roof, with the glued end on the first line up from the eaves, and spread the glued fibres out to a width of about 1in (25mm) or so, working the glue in, and onto the roof surface with the plastic knife.

5   Repeat this process, laying the next bunch of cut and glued ends onto the second line up from the eaves, and continue up to the ridge. Decide which ridge form you want, as this will affect where the glue is placed on the last bunch. (*See* Fig 4.35. Method 1 shows the fibres from each side of the roof turned over and intertwined, while Method 2 shows a simple butt joint.)

6   Start with the next bundle at the eaves, working upwards as before. Repeat each row until the whole roof is covered.

7   When the roof is covered, and the glue is completely dry, give it all a brush to blend the fibres together, and cut off the surplus fibres at the eaves, being particularly careful to achieve the correct angle of cut. (*See* Fig 4.35.)

8   In real roofs, strands of hazel or willow were used to fix the thatch down in certain places. These strands are called 'liggers'. To make them for your dolls' house roof, cut thin strips of balsa wood and colour them to match the thatch. Fix them through the coconut fibre to the underlying board or plywood, using as unobtrusive a pin or tack as possible. Quite often, two liggers were placed parallel and near to the eaves, but the patterns made by liggers vary greatly from region to region. For an authentic pattern, look at roofs in your chosen area, or refer to good photos in books.

Chapter 5
The period chapters

The following chapters have been grouped according to popular names given to the periods covering reigning monarchs. This is a somewhat artificial grouping because historical happenings, especially those pertaining to social history, of which architecture is one aspect, do not conform tidily with specific dates. They generally develop in a slow manner, taking in various influences as they proceed. However, given these limitations, this method of grouping gives a broad indication of history adequate for the dolls' house enthusiast to pursue historical aspects of their hobby in sufficient detail.

Adapting buildings

In the periods from the late sixteenth century onwards, there were times when domestic building on a grand scale took place. It would be interesting to visit some of these houses to study the details and furnishings of the period, some of which could be used in a fashionable dolls' house. However, these great houses are rather too large to be translated into 1/12 scale in their entirety, so, as mentioned before, it is the smaller houses that are being considered in this book. There are many delightful small houses in every period which can be adapted to dolls' house size, and these show many of the design details incorporated in the grand houses, albeit in a simplified form.

Dating buildings

It is not always easy to date buildings because there can be a wide variation between those in different areas. This can be confusing when you are trying to reproduce details accurately, but remember that any advanced ideas in design and construction took a long time to reach rural areas, so buildings in such places could be as much as 50 years behind those in towns as far as design, construction and standards of comfort are concerned. There was little communication between town and country until the eighteenth and nineteenth centuries, and even then it was limited. The development of printing in the sixteenth century spread ideas, but many people could not read or write, so these ideas were only available to people who had money or learning, and who would be living in growing centres of industry and commerce. If you do want to find out the date of a particular building, try to visit the county library or contact any local history society.

Another point to remember when considering what details to use in a building, is that people altered their houses over the years to conform with fashion. For example, when the sash window became popular in Georgian times, some owners of Stuart manor houses took out their traditional casement windows and replaced them with the new sashes. So, you can be flexible with the history of your house if you wish!

The plans

In each period chapter there are illustrations showing a selection of buildings as they would have appeared at the time. I would emphasise that these are just selections of the many variations of design and construction that are to be found in different parts of England, and you may wish to investigate these further.

Plans of some of the buildings shown are included in each chapter. These are all drawn to approximately the same scale as far as room sizes and heights are concerned, but wall thicknesses are shown diagrammatically. In reality, walls can vary in thickness from 13½in (340mm) to 18in (460mm) in brick, while those of stone can be anything from 24in (610mm) upwards. Half-timbered walls are only the thickness of the timber framing, together with the external and internal finishes.

Notes are given on how to adapt the plans to suit simple dolls' house layouts. Such adaptations can involve the use of false doors. These are usually in the back wall of a dolls' house and, as their name suggests, indicate a door to a room beyond. False doors are thus very useful as they can show the disposition of rooms in a house, without the need for constructing them. In a small Victorian house, for instance, such a door could indicate the back kitchen or scullery. A Georgian mansion could have a door or doors apparently leading from a front reception room to an inner salon. By using false doors, your house can show that it has several rooms, just through suggestion.

Notes are also given, at the end of each chapter, for making 1/12 scale models with effects particularly relevant to that period.

Chapter 6
The Tudor period

The word 'Tudor' always strikes a chord in those of us who are interested in the history of buildings, whether that interest lies in full-size or miniature ones. Depending on where you live, the picture conjured up is of a house built either of timber with plaster panels, or of mellow stone. Such buildings were put up by the wealthier people of Tudor times; the homes of peasants and poorer people have long since disappeared or fallen into disrepair.

Historical background

The Tudor period began with the accession of Henry VII in 1485, after the Battle of Bosworth Field, and ended with the death of Queen Elizabeth I in 1603. The period takes its name from the Welsh Henry Tudor – Henry VII – who was born in Pembroke Castle in 1457. In 1486, he married Elizabeth of York, thus linking the houses of York and Lancaster and bringing to an end the Wars of the Roses.

The population of England at the time of Henry's accession was about 2½ million. One-tenth of these people lived in towns which were little more than what we now think of as large villages. London was an overcrowded place, surrounded by fields within walking distance of its centre. The Midlands and the south of England were covered in deciduous woodland – mainly oak – with clearings for villages, hamlets and farms. Hills, moorlands and fens made up the north.

Government

Henry VII was a good administrator and governed wisely, although he did have a streak of avarice in his make-up. During his reign, the material wealth of the country increased. His foreign policy was such that England was respected abroad. Overseas trade was stimulated and, near home, treaties were made with the Flemish people who needed English wool for their cloth industry.

When Henry VII died, he left a firm and wealthy monarchy for his successor. The feudal system of the Middle Ages had declined and a considerable part of the population was now made up of people with smallholdings, tradesmen, and craftsmen, including carpenters, weavers and smiths. Wool, which in the late fifteenth century was exported to Europe, was now, in the early sixteenth century, used in the production of English cloth. Increased sheep rearing made landowners rich and able to build more elaborate houses of timber and stone.

Industry

While the industries of tin mining in Cornwall and coal mining in the north started to develop, it was in the heavily wooded areas of the south that the English landscape drastically altered, for several reasons. Henry VIII was responsible for the development of the Navy on a large scale. Ship building required vast quantities of timber, mainly oak. Coupled with the growing iron industry which needed charcoal for smelting, these requirements made inroads into the forests of the south of England. Towards the end of the Tudor period, Queen Elizabeth herself issued warnings against the use of timber for non-essential work, and this resulted in less timber being used for building framework. In turn, plastered panels became larger than had been the practice in mid-Tudor times, in the homes of wealthy yeomen and merchants. (Early Tudor houses also used less timber, but this was because their owners were not wealthy enough to afford it.) The west and north-west of England did not use timber for smelting because the ore was not plentiful as it was in the south-east, and ship building was not carried on to the same extent as it was in the south where suitable oak was locally available; therefore, half-timbered houses in the west and north-west incorporated decorative motifs in their designs.

Villages expanded into small towns, and by the end of Elizabeth's reign, the population of England was about 4 million.

Plans

The main type of plan found in large and medium-sized houses of the early Tudor period consisted of a hall, extending through the height of two storeys, and flanked by rooms at ground and first floor levels. The fire was placed centrally in the hall, and smoke went out through the roof. These houses were known as 'hall houses' and continued to be built in remote areas right through the fifteenth, sixteenth and early seventeenth centuries.

This type of plan was characteristic of rural areas where the house would stand in its own field or garden, and the small landowner or tenant would grow vegetables and other plants, and, if space permitted, raise domestic animals. In some areas, a plan evolved for houses known as long houses. The accommodation for the occupiers was similar to that of the hall house, but one end was extended to form a cattle-byre or shippon. Developments in social conditions, however, eventually led to the cattle being housed in

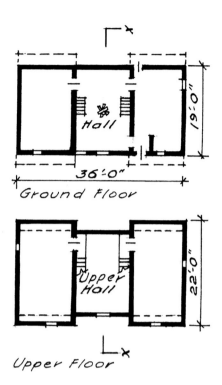

Ground Floor

Upper Floor

separate farm buildings. Long houses survived in moorland and upland areas where the usual building material was stone, but in other areas, where the material was not so durable, the cattle-byre forming part of the house was allowed to fall into disrepair.

Hall house plans were long and narrow, based on a bay width of 12ft (370cm) to 14ft (430cm). (A bay was the distance between roof trusses.) Houses could be three or four bays long, and quite large. This was especially so after about 1500, with the rise of small scale landowners and tenant farmers. In the south-east particularly, their half-timbered construction made a considerable impact on the rural landscape.

Because a dolls' house 56in (142cm) long might be too large for a limited space, you could look around for a smaller hall house on which to base your design. These, generally, were earlier than the larger houses, built by less wealthy people who could not afford to use so much timber in their design. There are many examples of these smaller houses in east Kent.

Another possibility for the dolls' house builder is to construct a hall house built on a narrow town site. As the sixteenth century progressed and towns grew, town sites became more restricted than those in the countryside. The owners were usually shopkeepers or craftsmen, and their homes usually comprised domestic premises over shops or workshops. These buildings spread upwards instead of outwards. The shop might have a two-storey hall backing onto it, while a side passage led to a courtyard with the kitchen beyond, to reduce the risk of fire.

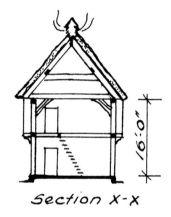

Section X-X

Fig 6.1 An early Tudor house in Sussex, about 1500. Less timber was used than 50 years later, when greater wealth enabled more use of it. The windows have wooden mullions (uprights) to support shutters, or sheets of oiled paper or horn. The two-storey hall has a central log fire, with the smoke going up through louvres in the roof, which is made of thatch. Stairs lead from the hall to the upper rooms by way of small landings.

Plans and section of Fig 6.1.

Hall

Drain

SHIPPON

42'-0"

27'-0"

16'-0"

Section B-B

20'-0"

Fig 6.2 An early Tudor hall house on Dartmoor, built of roughly-dressed granite blocks from the moor. The windows have wooden mullions to support shutters. The two-storey hall has a central fire, the smoke going up through louvres in the thatched roof. The porch has stone slates, found locally. Known as a long house, this included a cattle-byre or shippon built alongside the dwelling area, as indicated on the plans.

Plans and section of Fig 6.2.

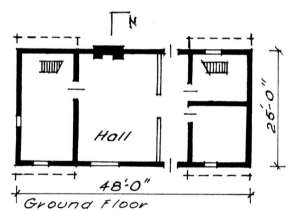

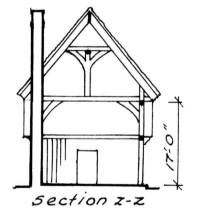

Fig 6.3 A Kentish yeoman's hall house, built around 1550, showing close half-timbering, and glass in the leaded casement windows. The brick fireplace is at the back, continues through the full height of the two-storey hall, and extends its brickwork into a stack through the roof. Stairs lead from lower rooms to upper rooms. The roof is of tiles, hand-made from the local brick earths.

Plans and section of Fig 6.3.

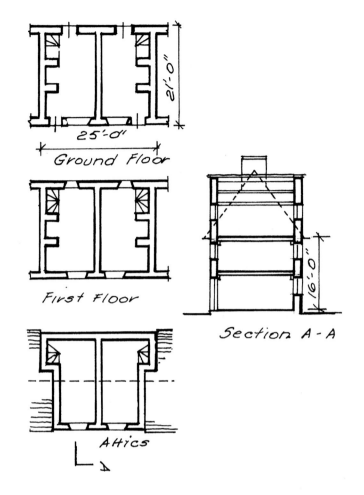

Fig 6.4 A late-sixteenth-century pair of town houses in Dorset, built of Portland stone, and with glazed, leaded casement windows. The roofs are covered with stone slabs, probably from the Purbeck area.

Plans and section of Fig 6.4.

When these town houses were built of timber, as the majority were at this time (the exception being in stone areas where timber was not readily available), it was a fairly easy matter to extend upwards for two or three, or even more storeys. The way in which this was done formed a characteristic element of half-timbered buildings on restricted sites. The carpenter used a jetty which enabled each storey to overhang the one beneath in such a way as to stabilize the whole structure. (*See* Fig 6.8.) The jetty was also used in some country homes so that some rooms on the upper floor overhung those on the ground floor.

With the development of these multi-storey town buildings in later Tudor times, the question of access to the upper floors had to be considered; the multi-flight staircase developed in conjunction with the flooring over the hall at first floor level.

In some areas, the planning arrangements of rooms in moderately-sized hall houses was altered by the use of brick for building chimney stacks and fireplaces. The exit for smoke was now incorporated in a fireplace, and the stack placed at the rear or side of the two-storey hall. These new arrangements in the late sixteenth century were continued into the seventeenth century, when they developed into the comfortable living styles of the Stuart period.

Fig 6.5 A merchant's town house, about 1595, based on the hall house, but modified to suit a narrow site, with the hall now floored over at the first-floor level. It is of half-timber construction. This example is typical of the west and north-west, with its extra decorative pieces of timber. The chimney stack rises from the brick fireplace at the back of the hall. The roof covering is local stone slabs. If stone slabs were unavailable, the roof would be thatch, plastered to resist the spread of fire.

Plans and section of Fig 6.5.

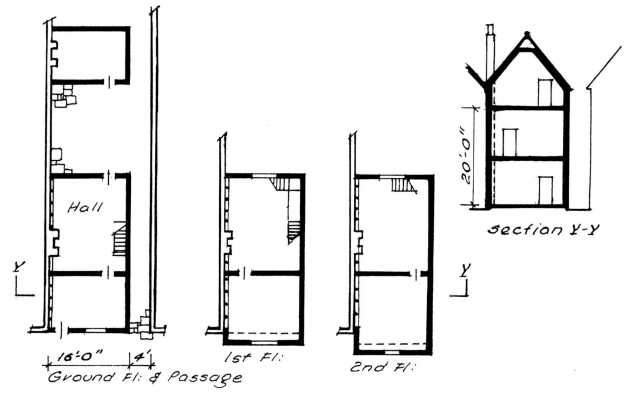

Hall

16'0" 4'
Ground Fl: & Passage

1st Fl:

2nd Fl:

20'-0"

section Y-Y

Hints on adapting the plans

Figures 6.1, 6.2 and 6.3

The plans of the houses shown in Figs 6.1 and 6.3 can be used as they are shown because they are one room deep. The long house, shown in Fig 6.2, can also be built as shown, with its shippon. The shippon would be built of similar granite blocks to those used in the dwelling area, with ventilating holes, one of which is shown on the elevation, and the positions of which are shown on the plan. The roof would be thatched. However, if this makes the building too long, the house could be used on its own, with the opening to the shippon made solid at the house end.

Figure 6.4

The plan of the building shown in Fig 6.4 could be used as it is to give two small town houses. Alternatively, it could be adapted to form one house by omitting the front and back doors and the staircase to one house, introducing access doors into the ground and first floor cross walls, and omitting the attic cross wall entirely.

Figure 6.5

The plan of the merchant's house, shown in Fig 6.5, could be cut off at one room deep, with false doors at the back showing access to the upper floors. (*See* the section on The Plans in Chapter 5.) The ground floor can be laid out as a shop or workshop.

Walls

Walls were generally built of a timber framework, or, alternatively of stone or a form of compacted earth. Towards the end of the period, brick was used for building the large houses of aristocrats, but it was used in small houses only in the construction of fireplaces and chimney stacks.

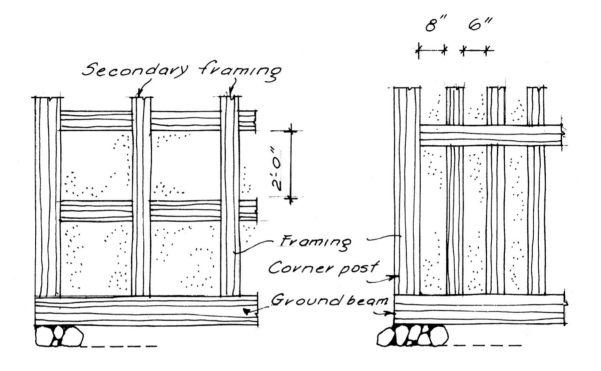

Above **Fig 6.6 The two main types of half-timbered wall construction used square or narrow panels.**

Right **Fig 6.7 Half-timbered wall construction, with additional decorative members.**

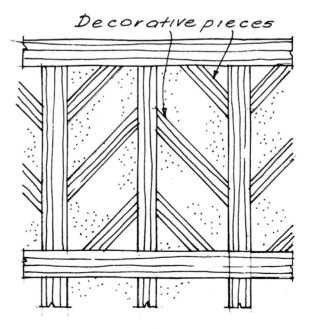

Top right **Fig 6.8** Jettied construction, looking up.

Bottom right **Fig 6.9** Wattle and daub panel.

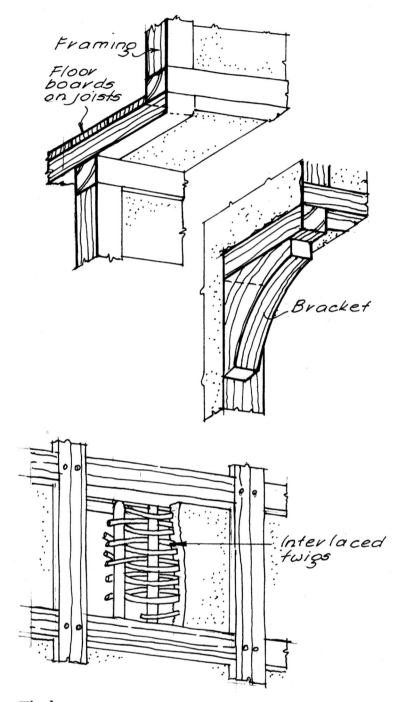

Framing

Floor boards on joists

Bracket

Interlaced twigs

Timber framing

■ The different types of timber framing might interest someone who would like to construct a whole framework, perhaps leaving part of it on display as a half-built house, alongside one already completed. There are many books about the history and construction of timber-framed houses which will interest an enthusiast. (*See* Bibliography, page 139.)

■ The type of timber-framed house which usually appeals to the dolls' house enthusiast is one which dates from about 1500 onwards, built by a merchant or yeoman who could afford glass in his windows. Such a house would have the roof timbers showing in the hall and upper rooms and while this construction might be interesting to some dolls' house builders, you might prefer to follow the developments of the early seventeenth century, when a floor was inserted into the two-storey hall, and beamed ceilings were constructed in the upper rooms.

Timber

The design of timber-framed buildings varied in different parts of England. (*See* the section on Timber in Chapter 3.)

The sizes of timbers and panels varied considerably. The ground beam could be 12 x 9in (305 x 230mm), or even 12 x 12in (305 x 305mm). Main corner posts could be 7in (178mm), 8in (203mm) or 9in (23mm) square. Secondary timber uprights could be 4 or 5in (102 or 127mm) deep, and 5 or 6in (127 or 152mm) across. Panels could be 24in (610mm) square, as shown in Fig 6.6, 24 x 15in (610 x 380mm), or, where very narrow, 6 to 8in (152 to 203mm).

The stability of a timber-framed house was derived from the size, disposition and jointing of the timber members themselves. The infill panels between the timbers of the wall framework did not play any part in supporting the main structure; the timbers were able to carry lightweight infill panels of plaster and woven twigs (wattle and daub), and also glazed casement windows. (*See also* the section on Plans.)

Stone

The stability of stone houses depended on the thickness of their external walls and the way in which these were tied in to cross walls; they were usually built to a maximum of two storeys, sometimes with dormer windows in the roofs. The same basic construction of thick, load-bearing walls was applied to important stone and brick buildings – brick became widely used in the time of Henry VIII and this use continued on through that of Elizabeth I, and into the time of the Stuarts.

Small stone buildings showed differences in their details, according to whether the stone was easy or difficult to work, and whether the owner was wealthy enough to afford the labour entailed. (*See* Fig 4.14; *see also* Fig 6.18.)

Compacted earth

Compacted earth was used in the construction of small cottages in districts where timber was not available and stone was too expensive to transport. It had to be protected from the weather, so roofs of thatch were laid with overhanging eaves, and bases of walls were built on rough stone or pebbles, or later, on brick. Corners of walls were rounded to minimize damage from passing farm carts. This compacted earth was usually clay or chalk mixed with water, and strengthened with pebbles, straw or other organic material. It was used for the construction of small buildings in country areas until the eighteenth century. (It is difficult to date such buildings with accuracy, so I have included examples in Chapter 10: Small cottages, where the emphasis is on local materials rather than age.)

Brick

Where bricks were used they varied in size through the period but generally, were about 2in (51mm) thick by 8½ to 9½in (216 to 241mm) long. The dimension of 2in (51mm) (thinner than those generally used today, which are a little less than 2¾in (70mm)), enabled the bricks to dry more evenly, which was important as they were made from very wet clays, and dried in uncontrolled conditions. Bricks were uneven and required thick mortar joints to align them in courses; these joints could be ½in (13mm) thick in places. Bricks were laid rather randomly, or in variations of English bond. (*See* Fig 6.10.)

Fig 6.10 Tudor brickwork.

Roofs and chimneys

In early Tudor times, small houses were roofed with thatch or with thin pieces of oak, called shingles. (These were laid in a similar way to tiles, which made their appearance later in the period.)

Thatch

Because the plans of small houses were simple rectangles, thatching was simple, covering a gabled or hipped construction. (*See* Fig 2.6.) The thatching of simple Tudor houses was rather roughly done and did not bear any resemblance to the sophisticated and decorative designs of later periods, some of which followed complicated roof designs. Where thatch was used on these roofs, it was laid with many ridges and valleys and undulating eave lines which swept over dormer windows.

When London started to expand in mid Tudor times, new buildings there were not allowed to be thatched. Tiles were becoming available, and existing thatched roofs were covered with a lime-based plaster to reduce the risk of fire. This practice of limewashing eventually spread to other parts of England.

Tiles

Tiles, like bricks, first appeared in the south-east around 1500, and were used on yeomen's and merchants' houses in that area. Other areas continued to use thatch, thin stone slabs or local slates on small buildings. Large buildings dating from the mid Tudor period until its end, were roofed with tiles, stone slabs or slates, and sometimes sheets of cast lead were used.

Fireplaces

As mentioned under Plans, early Tudor houses, with their two-storey halls, had a central fireplace which was open to a hole in the roof. After about 1500, when bricks became available in some areas, the fireplace was moved to the back or side of the hall and connected to an external stack. Brick was also used in stone areas if it could be transported easily, because it was more fire-resistant than some types of stone.

Chimneys

The large aristocratic houses of the time showed an abundance of decorative chimney stacks. This was particularly so in brick areas, because bricks were so easy to cut or mould into patterns. Chimney stacks at Hampton Court in Surrey and Chenies Manor in Buckinghamshire show examples of these. They are rather exuberant for the smaller houses of the time, but if you wish to have splendid stacks on your wealthy yeoman's house, why not? Just make them fairly simple and in keeping with your building. (An idea for making a decorative stack is shown at the end of this

Chimney pots

Because most dolls' houses come supplied with chimney pots, they can either be dispensed with in your Tudor house, or the house can be peopled with Georgian folk or a modern family both of whom may well have added pots.

chapter; *see* Fig 6.23.) Stone chimney stacks of the mid and late Tudor period show restrained ornament in the form of elegant mouldings, which give interest to the stack.

From the thirteenth century there had been several devices to improve draught in chimneys, but the separate, circular chimney pots as we know them today, were not generally used until the time of King George III, and then they did not project more than 2in (51mm) above the stack, so as not to be visible from the ground.

Below left **Fig 6.11 A pair of grand stone chimney stacks.**

Below **Fig 6.12 Decorative brick chimney stacks.**

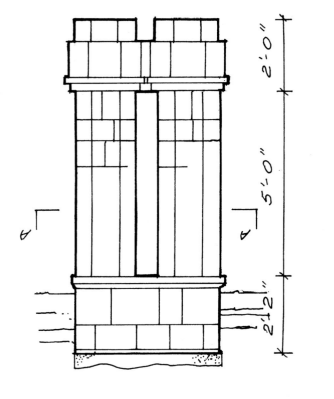

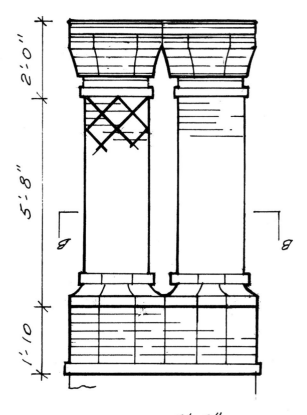

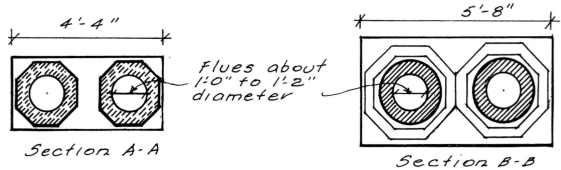

Flues about 1'-0" to 1'-2" diameter

Section A-A

Section B-B

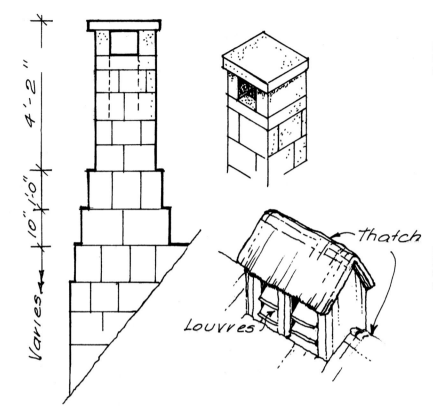

Fig 6.13 A sixteenth-century single stone stack. A stone slab was placed over the flue to stop rain coming in.

Fig 6.14 In early Tudor hall houses, a louvred opening was built on the roof to allow smoke from the fire to escape.

Windows

Below **Fig 6.15** An early window with timber uprights. This could take sheets of oiled paper or pieces of horn, or could be protected by internal sliding shutters.

Below right **Fig 6.16** Detail of the construction of glazed casement windows.

Windows in early Tudor houses were unglazed because only the wealthy could afford glass in their windows. The beautiful stained glass found in mediaeval churches was paid for by the King or Church authorities. The early unglazed domestic windows or 'wind-eyes' were either provided with upright timbers to which sheets of oiled linen or pieces of horn were fixed, or had provision for internal shutters.

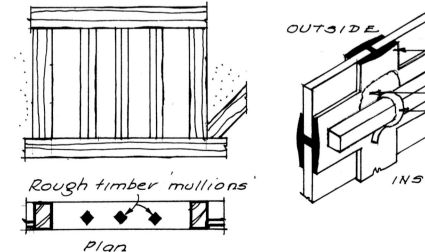

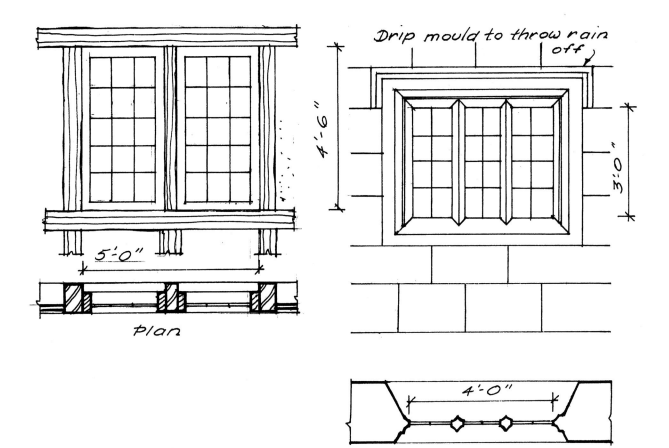

Plan

Plan

Casement windows

By the mid-sixteenth century, builders of small and medium-sized houses could afford window glass, although it was only obtainable in small pieces. These pieces were now used in the making of the typical Tudor casement window. Each casement was made from a wrought iron frame, which was fixed to the surrounding woodwork or stonework. Horizontal strengthening bars, called saddle bars, were fixed to this frame at intervals, possibly by an old form of rivetting. The frame was then filled with small pieces of glass, which were joined together with strips of lead called cames, and attached to the saddle bars by means of copper wire ties embedded in lead bosses: these secured the lead cames at suitable junctions. Casement windows could either be fixed or made to open. A fixed window had one frame set into the stone or wood surround, while an opening window had an additional inner frame which was hinged to the outer frame, sometimes with a pivot hinge.

In a timber-framed house, the framing formed the load-bearing structure, and it was relatively easy to insert windows where they were required, but it was difficult to insert large windows in a solid, load-bearing wall of brick or stone. So, windows remained small until later Tudor times, when intermediate structural pieces called mullions (verticals), and transomes (horizontals), were introduced

Left **Fig 6.17** Glazed casement windows set in a timber-framed building.

Above **Fig 6.18** Glazed casement windows set in a stone building.

Simulating casement windows

It is not necessary for the dolls' house builder to attempt this complicated construction; simply showing the window divided into small oblong or diamond-shaped panes will produce the desired effect. Soldered wire gives a realistic appearance, but, if soldering does not appeal, a simple method is given at the end of this chapter.

into the window area. Because it was easy to introduce windows into timber-framed houses, some of these developed with elaborate bays, especially in towns and in the homes of wealthy merchants.

Very wealthy people used glass to advertise their riches, and there are several Elizabethan examples of this. For instance, Hardwick Hall, built in 1591, was said to have 'more glass than wall'. It was built by Elizabeth Shrewsbury, known as 'Bess of Hardwick', who was a very rich woman, second only to Queen Elizabeth I herself in terms of wealth.

Dormer windows

The Tudor builders were also responsible for introducing the dormer window, called thus because, originally, it was a window that let light in to the sleeping apartment, or dormitory, of a monastic establishment. This type of window varied in character throughout England, depending on the type of house and the region in which it was built.

External doors

The type of oak-planked door widely used in small and medium-sized houses, was that constructed from a number of vertical planks fixed to three horizontal planks on the inside. Sometimes the vertical boards were butted together and the joints covered with moulded strips of wood. In other cases, the vertical planks were cut from radial-sawn oak, which meant that each one tapered slightly; the thin edge of each plank was tucked into a slit in the thick edge of the adjoining one, and the whole nailed together. This made the door draught-proof and gave it a slightly ridged surface.

Iron studs were sometimes used instead of nails to secure the planks in very heavy doors; you can see examples of these studs in old church doors. Domestic doors were usually hung on long, wrought iron hinges and were closed with a wooden latch operated

Simulating oak-planked doors
Attempting to tuck in and nail the planks at 1/12 scale can give clumsy results: it is sufficient to butt square-edged planks together. (*See* point C, Hints on achieving Tudor effects, at the end of this chapter.)

Fig 6.19 Outside and inside faces of a planked door. The size of planked doors varied, and strap hinges could be fixed to either face, depending on which way the door opened.

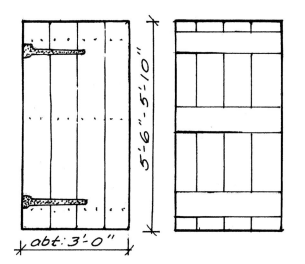

by a string from outside. A long bar secured the door inside against intruders – the well-known Suffolk latch did not appear until the eighteenth century. (A Suffolk latch is a wrought iron thumb latch, with a handle and lever going through the door to raise a latch on the other side when the thumb plate is pressed.)

Door frames were plain and simple, usually square-headed, although the 'Tudor arch' was sometimes incorporated, and lintels were sometimes carved.

Arranging studs

If you would like iron studs on your Tudor dolls' house door, find examples and study their arrangement carefully so that you can place your 'studs' in a realistic pattern.

Below Fig 6.20 A planked door set in the stone surround of a Tudor manor house.

Right Fig 6.21 A planked door set in a half-timbered surround.

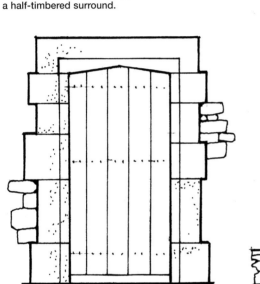

Metalwork

The work of the village smith in Tudor times was mainly directed towards utilitarian objects. Those used in the building trade for external work included hinges and the frames and fittings of casement windows. (*See* the section on Casement Windows, under Windows in this chapter.)

Gutters and downpipes

Owners of the larger Elizabethan houses started to install rainwater gutters and downpipes. Early gutters were sometimes made of wood, usually elm, but later ones were made from cast lead. These discharged into cast lead rainwater heads and downpipes. The heads were often decorated with a date or ornamental device.

Fig 6.22 Lead rainwater head and downpipe belonging to the Tudor period, as indicated by the date, but typical of the early Stuarts.

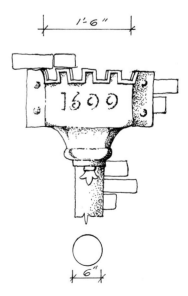

Hints on achieving Tudor effects

A

Look at joints, and where timbers meet in timber construction. Do not use a dark stain or paint plaster a bright white: it is generally believed that the black-and-white buildings of the west and north-west were painted this way in Victorian times. Give the timber and plaster a weathered look by rubbing in dilute colour or pencil. Make the bases of the buildings look grubby – the state of the roads in Tudor times left much to be desired.

B

For carvings on buildings, find some embossed paper or some lace or braid of a suitable design, stick it on the woodwork, and paint it, carefully pushing the paint well into the crevices. Lace and braid give the sharpest result.

C

For planked doors, scribing a single piece of wood to imitate planks is a simple alternative to using separate pieces butted together.

D

Small, leaded panes of glass can be imitated by cutting very thin strips of grey paper and sticking them onto acrylic sheet.

E

The chimney stack shown in Fig 6.23 was made from various shapes cut from card, glued together, and covered with brick paper. The top and middle flat pieces were made from octagonal shapes, with a black circle painted in the middle of the top piece, to represent the hollow centre of the flue. The model measures 5½in (140mm) high, but this can easily be altered.

Fig 6.23 Scale chimney stack, made using card and brick paper.

Chapter 7
The Stuart period

T he phrase 'Stuart period' is not one that immediately conjures up a picture of any specific type of house for the dolls' house enthusiast, but pick out a part such as Jacobean, William and Mary, or Queen Anne, or mention the name Christopher Wren, and the whole period comes to life.

Historical background

Historically, the Stuart period came between the somewhat flamboyant late Tudor time and the classicism of the early Georgians. As far as dates can be applied to the period, it extended from the accession of James I in 1603, until the end of Queen Anne's reign in 1714. However, socially and in the field of architecture, transition from one period to another was gradual and developed slowly. The Tudor Elizabethan style developed into that part of the Stuart period known as Jacobean, while the later years of the Stuart period saw the influences of the classical tradition. In between was the time of the Commonwealth (1649 until 1660), which ended with the recall of the exiled Charles II.

Developments in housing

The Elizabethan age had engendered more prosperity in certain classes of people, especially merchants and yeomen. Merchants were townspeople while yeomen were small-scale owners of land or tenant farmers. This prosperity generally continued throughout the Stuart period, although it experienced the usual setbacks due to political and social influences. Those people who prospered on a small scale could now afford to build their homes of more substantial materials than before, and this is why so many of our smaller and interesting houses date from the seventeenth century.

Foreign influences

Many of the grander houses being built at this time showed foreign influences. These influences slowly drifted into country areas from the more sophisticated towns, where the architects of the time were

Fig 7.1 This house shows the use of brick, which was widespread in the seventeenth century, together with Dutch influence in the design of the gables. The casement windows have diamond-shaped panes, which were also common in the preceding Tudor period. The Stuarts often used small, rectangular panes of glass as well. There is a small decorative stone panel between the windows on the first floor. The roof is covered with hand-made clay tiles, and has a double pitch to cover the greater depth of the house. The plan shows the increase in the number of rooms thought to be desirable for a medium-sized residence at this time.

using them. They included influences from France, dating from the return of Charles II from his exile, and Dutch influences from the time of the accession of William and Mary. Classical motifs were also used in the design of important buildings. The classical influence reached England from Italy, mainly through illustrations in architectural books by Italian architects. Eventually, simplified versions of these motifs were adopted by local builders and craftsmen in small towns and villages.

Architecture

The seventeenth century saw the rise of architecture as a profession in its own right – previously, building design had come within the province of other trades and professions. Eminent architects of the time include Inigo Jones (1573–1652), Hugh May (1622–1684) and Christopher Wren (1632–1723).

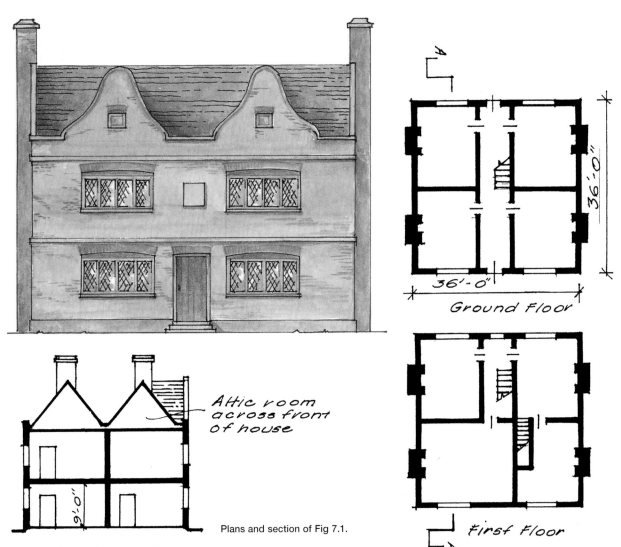

Ground Floor

Attic room across front of house

Plans and section of Fig 7.1.

Section A-A

First Floor

Plans

The two-storeyed hall house, typical of the preceding Tudor period, was still being built in some remote areas. However, the desire for more privacy and a greater number of rooms, which had become usual in Elizabethan times, led to a general modification of this

Fig 7.2 This house, in a country town in the south of England, was built around 1700. It is of brown brick, with red rubbed-brick window arches, and has a clay-tiled roof of double span, with dormer windows. (Such a house may also have been built with red brick, but the colour would not have been as bright as the red brick in the window arches.) The house has a classical entrance door, wooden eaves and details, and sash windows, which were becoming popular. In areas where the use of stone was traditional, a similar house could have been built in finely-dressed stone, with a stone-slated roof. The eaves would have been constructed either of wood, or of stone with simple mouldings.

Plans and section of Fig 7.2.

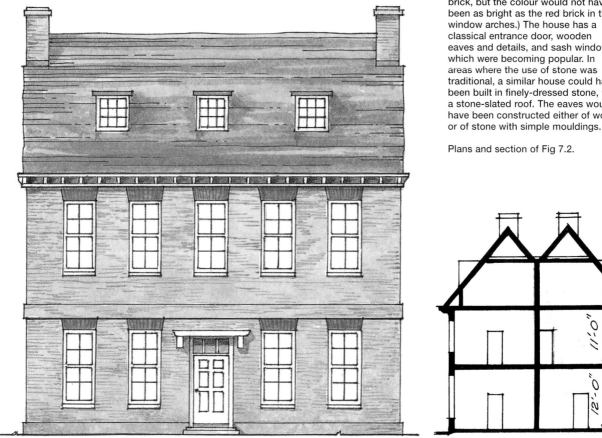

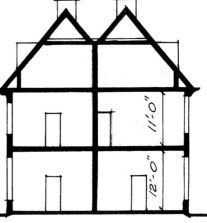

Section B-B

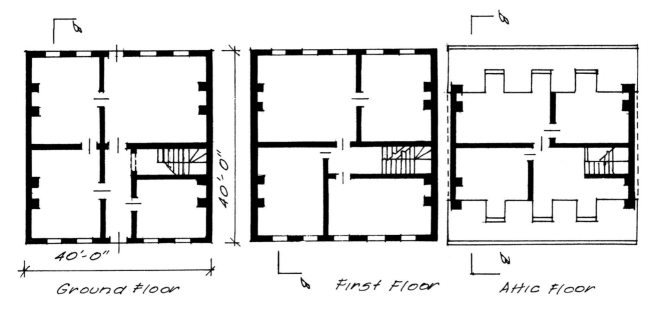

40'-0"

40'-0"

Ground Floor

First Floor

Attic Floor

plan. In the late sixteenth and early seventeenth centuries, a first floor with a ceiling was introduced and the central hole in the roof, for the escape of smoke, was abolished. This alteration, based on social needs, ran parallel to the more general use of brick, which enabled chimney stacks and fireplaces to be constructed. These were built on the rear or side walls of the ground and first floors. In stone areas, while lovely stone fireplace surrounds were built, flues were lined with brick where possible, because it was more resistant to heat than some varieties of stone.

This introduction of more rooms, leading to a different distribution of fireplaces and chimney stacks, influenced the external appearance of a house.

Fig 7.3 This Cotswold farmhouse differs little in its external appearance from a late Tudor one in the same area. However, classical motifs are creeping in, as reflected in the ball finials on the main gables. The house is built of Cotswold limestone blocks, lightly dressed, and laid in courses of varying widths. The roof is covered with slabs of the same material. The attic floor is approached by a small staircase from a room on the first floor.

Plans and section of Fig 7.3.

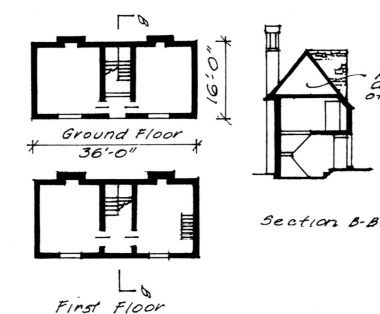

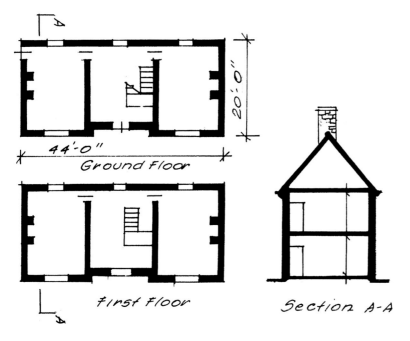

Fig 7.4 This is a mid- to seven-teenth-century stone farmhouse. It shows how local builders retained traditional features like the casement windows, while taking note of the classical influences, which can be seen in the design of the eaves (made of wood), and the entrance doorway. The centre part of the front is recessed, which was a popular classical design feature, intended to emphasize the front entrance. The house is built of dressed limestone blocks laid in courses, and has roofing slabs of the same material: these have darkened due to weathering, and the growth of mosses and lichens. Such a house would be found in the lowland farming area of the limestone belt in southern England.

Plans and section of Fig 7.4.

Setting aside the consideration of the new buildings in London from 1707, the designs of which were the forerunners of the early Georgian period, and showed the early extremes of classical influences (as seen in the Queen's House at Greenwich, by Inigo Jones), there were many houses typical of the Stuart period which epitomized a comfortable standard of living for that time. These developed from those of one room in depth, such as farmhouses (very suitable for the dolls' house builder), to those of a square or oblong plan, incorporating a large number of rooms, depending on the wealth or social standing of the owner.

Hints on adapting the plans

Figure 7.1

The front part of the house shown in Fig 7.1 can be used on its own, inserting a wall in the ground floor where the staircase goes up beyond, and inserting an archway with a curtain in this wall. False doors can be put in on the first floor. The front of the double-span roof sits nicely on this part.

Figure 7.2

The front part of the house shown in Fig 7.2 can be used on its own, with a full-length mirror placed on the wall opposite the staircase on the ground floor, to show its reflection through the archway. For this to work, the entrance corridor has to be wide enough to show an adequate reflection, so some experimenting with temporary pieces is advisable. You could also set the mirror at a slight angle. It will only be necessary to construct part of the staircase – that which will be reflected on the ground floor. Alternatively, you can pretend that the staircase is at the back of the house, add false doors, and make the front rooms larger on the ground, first and attic floors. Again, the front of the double-span roof can be used as shown.

Figures 7.3 and 7.4

The plans of Figs 7.3 and 7.4 can be used as shown.

Walls

The development of brick making and stone quarrying during the seventeenth century meant that brick and stone were the main materials used for new domestic buildings. In some regions, however, where brick and stone were not readily available, there were other materials used, especially for small houses. The tradition of timber-framing continued in many places, and in some parts of the west and north-west, many ornamental timbers were used to enrich the patterning of the walls. In other areas, and in small houses, the square panels of timber-framed buildings were still filled with the plain, plastered wickerwork (wattle and daub), that had been used in the sixteenth century. Brick was sometimes used as an infill between structural timbers, but this was a replacement where the plastered panel had deteriorated. In other places, especially East Anglia, houses were built from lightweight and roughly finished structural timbers, and wickerwork panels; these were both plastered over to form a smooth finish. This plaster surface was sometimes ornamented with incised or relief decoration, applied by hand and known as pargetting.

Fig 7.5 Seventeenth-century raised pargetting on a fifteenth-century timber-framed house in Suffolk.

Brick

Bricks had been used by the Romans, but the brick industry then died out in England until the thirteenth century, when limited quantities became available through Flemish immigrants introducing their methods. Until the seventeenth century, bricks had been used mainly for important buildings, but seventeenth-century merchants and yeomen who lived in the brick earth regions liked this material for building their homes, and created a demand for it. In the south and south-east especially, there was not as much timber available as there had been in Tudor times – much had gone for ship building and iron smelting – so the production of bricks was a growing industry.

This widening use of bricks was coupled with a growing awareness of the hazards of fire, especially after the Great Fire of London in 1666. Legislation was then introduced in London to restrict the construction of timber-framed buildings. So, in brick earth areas this material was widely used because of its cheapness due to its ready availability, and in areas where fire was a hazard it was used out of necessity. Sometimes old timber-framed houses were encased in a single thickness of bricks.

These practical aspects of the use of bricks eventually led to the realization that they were also attractive and, therefore, could be used in fashionable buildings. In fact, the latter part of the period saw the additional development of brickwork for purely ornamental purposes. One of these developments was the production of bricks called 'rubbers'. They were made softer than usual by adjusting the mix of clay and sand, and burning at a lower temperature. This meant that they could be cut to a shape and rubbed with another brick to give a smooth face and a fine joint. They became widely used in the ensuing Georgian period.

The brick bond in general use in the Stuart period was that known as Flemish, which gradually superseded the previous English bond. (*See* Figs 4.1 and 4.2.)

Stone

In areas where stone predominated, quarrying developed at this time. Stone was a more variable material than brick in its qualities of hardness, texture, size and colour, all of which affected the appearance of a building. The hardness and texture of bricks could generally be determined by the proportion of sand and clay in the raw mixture and by the burning process; the colour was the result of the minerals present in the particular brick earth, though there was some choice over which earth was used. The hardness and texture of stone could not be changed or influenced, the size depended both on how they occurred naturally and on the quarrying methods employed, and the shape depended on whether they were able to be sawn to a smooth finish, or only roughly dressed. As with bricks, the colour of stone depended on the minerals present.

Small houses in a village could be built either of roughly-dressed or sawn stone, but the large stone houses of wealthier people, were always built of large, sawn blocks. Roughly-dressed stone was stone direct from the quarry, roughly shaped and finished, although the degree of finish depended on the type of tools used and the amount of labour expended. (*See* the section on Stonework, under Walls in Chapter 4.)

Corner design

During the mid to late Stuart period, a popular design element was introduced in buildings built of brick; the corners (quoins) were built with projecting, chamfered stones (*see* Fig 7.6), or projecting brickwork (*see* Fig 7.7). Designs were also made in walls by recessing bricks to form panels.

Using textured sheets
When buying building papers or textured sheets, the dolls' house builder needs to ensure that Flemish bond is used for the Stuart period.

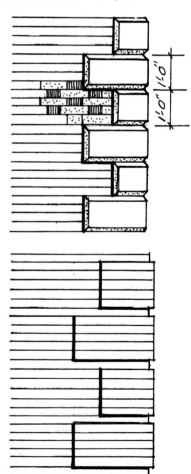

Fig 7.6 Projecting stone corners on a brick building. The edges were either chamfered, as shown, or plain.

Fig 7.7 Corners made from projecting brickwork.

Roofs and chimneys

Small houses in a village street and shops with living accommodation were often built tightly next to each other in a random way, making the best use of a small plot of land. The various heights of these buildings, together with the different roof ridge lines, create the varied outline of many of our village streets.

The terrace of houses, designed as a whole entity, did not develop until the eighteenth century was advanced, although its beginnings could be seen in London at the start of Queen Anne's reign in 1702. Merchants and other reasonably well-to-do people lived mainly in detached houses built from a considered design, probably thought out by a local builder. These houses generally had small gardens.

The plan of the detached Stuart house, as with any building, influenced the design of its roof. It could be seen from all sides; sometimes it had overhanging eaves – statutorily forbidden in London from 1707 – and sometimes the roof slope was seen peeping up from behind a parapet. (*See* Figs 7.8 and 7.9.)

Eaves

The important *Building Act* of 1707 made a great difference to the appearance of buildings in London. (*See also* the section on Sash Windows, under Windows in Chapter 7.) Hitherto, houses and shops had been built with overhanging wooden eaves – sometimes a very decorative feature. This was now considered a fire hazard, so all new buildings in London were required to take their solid external walls up beyond the eaves line to form a parapet. The Act referred to buildings in London only, but as London was the centre of fashion, this alteration in design was soon copied in some

Left **Fig 7.8** A late-seventeenth-century house, built around 1690, with the overhanging eaves characteristic of small houses of this time, and traditional casement windows with small, leaded panes.

Right **Fig 7.9** An early-eighteenth-century house with the parapet legally required in London after 1707, and sash windows, which were becoming popular. The window frames are set flush with the front face of the brick wall.

fashionable houses in other parts of the country, though overhanging wooden eaves continued to be constructed in many country homes well into the eighteenth century. Where stone was used and it was usual to build the eaves in that material, these too, eventually gave way to the parapet design.

Shape and span

The house with a single depth plan could be covered with a simple single-span roof. Those houses of greater depth had two small spans covering the area.

The increasing employment of servants led to a need for their living-in accommodation. The roof seemed to be a suitable place for this purpose, so dormer windows were widely used. The term 'dormer' refers to both an additional window built through a sloping roof (see Fig 7.2), or the development of a main wall into a miniature gable with a window in it (see Figs 7.1 and 7.3). Additional windows had little effect on the appearance of the roof, but gables gave the roof a distinctive shape.

Thatch

Thatch had always been the main roofing material for small 'village-type' houses, and it remained so throughout the seventeenth, eighteenth and nineteenth centuries. However, improvements in wagon transport during the seventeenth century did allow for a wider use of different materials, although these still had to be available relatively locally. Their delivery depended on the amount required and the distance to be travelled from quarry or tile works to the building site. The price had to include the conveyance of horse and driver there and back, usually for one day.

Tiles and slates

The detached farmhouse and Manor house buildings were now roofed with tiles or stone slates, or with slates themselves, depending on the locality. However, thatch was still used as an inexpensive roofing material, especially in the south, south-west and East Anglia. Slates were obtainable locally in the Lake District and Cornwall. These were irregular and in different colours, and were laid in diminishing courses – largest at the eaves and smallest at the ridge. Stone 'slates' were relatively thin slabs of stone which could be split easily; these were found in the Cotswolds, Sussex, Dorset, the Midlands and the Pennines – different colours in the different regions. (See also the section on Stone, under Building materials in Chapter 3.)

Pantiles started to be imported from Europe during this period. They were widely used in East Anglia, along the north-east coast, and around the Bridgewater area. (See the section on Roofing tiles in Chapter 3 for details.)

Gables

Brick and stone gables were often quite ornamental: these ornamental gables were known as Dutch gables, due to the influence of Netherlands traditions which were reaching England through its eastern ports. There were two main types - the first, which was actually called Dutch, had an outline designed with convex and concave curves, and the second, known as stepped or crow-stepped, had an outline just as its name suggests. Stepped gables had originally been introduced by Flemish immigrants in the fourteenth century. Such gables were widely used in Scotland throughout the sixteenth and seventeenth centuries, and appeared in England as well. Examples of the curved Dutch gable can mostly be seen near the ports of eastern England, though their influence did spread, and examples can be found in Sussex and Hertfordshire. William III also brought influences from his native country, Holland, during his reign between 1689-1702.

Below left **Fig 7.10** A brick gable from Suffolk. The bricks forming the curves would have been specially hand-moulded.

Bottom left **Fig 7.11** This gable from north Norfolk forms part of the chimney stack. Hand-moulded bricks delineate the gable from the flint wall. This design is typical of small seventeenth-century buildings of the region.

Below right **Fig 7.12** A gable from the stone belt of Lincolnshire, typical of late Tudor times and still popular in the early Stuart period.

Bottom right **Fig 7.13** A Sussex gable from around 1640, showing both curved and stepped gables, and with stone dressings on the main brick walls.

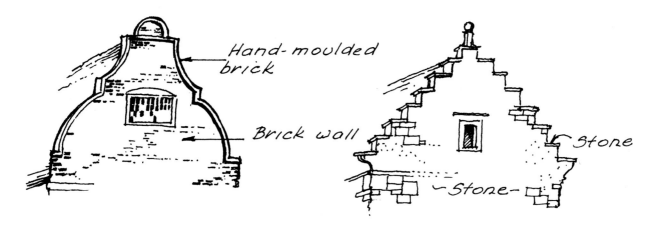

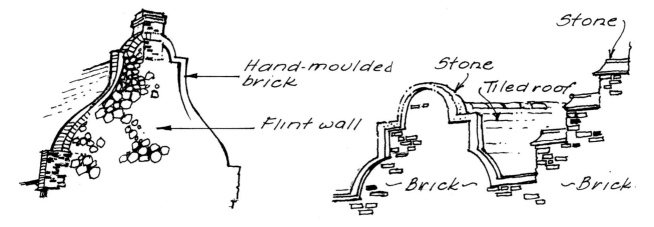

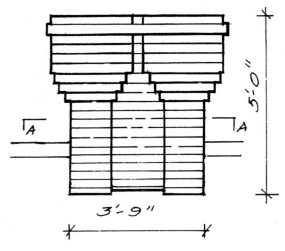

5'-0"

3'-9"

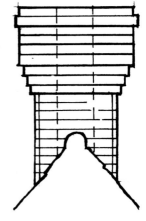

Fig 7.14 Brick chimney stack with ornamental recessed panels.

Side view

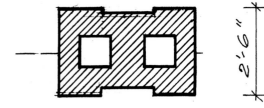

2'-6"

Plan on A-A

Fireplaces and chimney stacks

The different types of seventeenth-century plans naturally led to a varied disposition of fireplaces and chimney stacks. The stacks formed an important design element in Stuart houses. They were built of

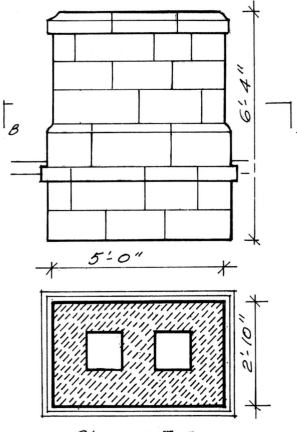

6'-4"

5'-0"

2'-10"

Plan on B-B

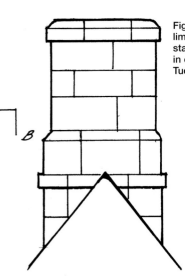

Fig 7.15 Chimney stack built from limestone. Both this stack, and the stack shown in Fig 7.9, have two flues, in contrast with the single stacks of Tudor times.

Side view

stone or brick, depending on the locality of the house, although, as in late Tudor times, bricks were sometimes brought from a distance because they withstood heat better than some stones. Flues were now grouped together to form simple rectangular stacks, as opposed to the single stacks of Tudor times.

Windows

Casement windows

The casement window used in the Tudor period developed in size and design during the seventeenth century. The early Stuart casement windows were similar to the late Tudor ones in that they consisted of wooden or stone surrounds with fixed or opening lights (the glazed areas of the windows). Strips of lead were still used to connect small pieces of glass, because glass was still relatively expensive and not obtainable in large pieces. (*See* the section on Windows in Chapter 6 for details of construction.) Where the Stuarts now required large windows, they incorporated more timber or stone mullions and transomes. However, with the widening use of brick as a walling material in the medium-sized house of Stuart times, a method was introduced whereby the brick wall was carried over the window opening by means of a brick arch. This arch rested on a shaped wooden piece made as part of the window frame. Ordinary bricks were used to form the arch itself, the shape being made by adjusting the width of the mortar joints. (Soft bricks, called rubbers, came into use in some Stuart buildings,

Below left **Fig 7.16** A window from the Stuart period with stone mullions and a transome, set in a stone wall. It is very similar to a Tudor window in detail, but is larger because of the transome which has been incorporated.

Below right **Fig 7.17** A wooden-framed window set in a brick wall. The arch is made from ordinary bricks, set at an angle over a shaped piece of timber. The mortar joints were wider at the top edge of the arch than at the bottom.

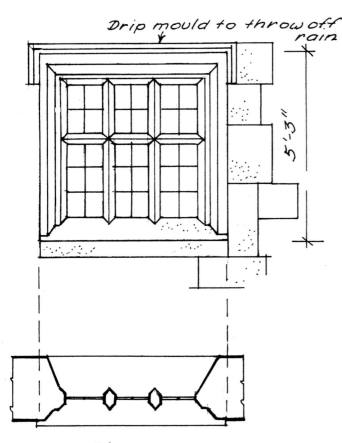

Drip mould to throw off rain

5'-3"

Plan

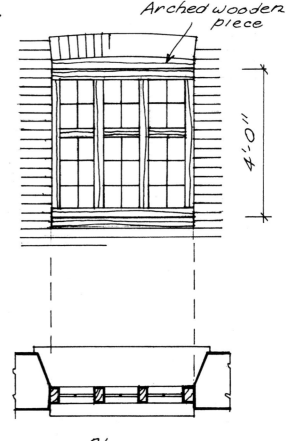

Arched wooden piece

4'-0"

Plan

but they were a main feature of the Georgian period, where their use enabled a flat arch to be constructed. (*See* Fig 8.1.)

The small casement window continued to be installed in buildings like farmhouses and cottages right up to, and including, Victorian times. One of the reasons for this continuing tradition was that, generally, ceiling heights in these smaller houses were rather low and would not permit the building in of a sash window which was tall in proportion to its width, although adaptations of the style can sometimes be seen in small houses. (These adaptations included unequally-sized vertically sliding sashes, so that the window fitted into a square opening.)

Fig 7.18 Sash windows, made of softwood and painted, were becoming popular in Stuart times.

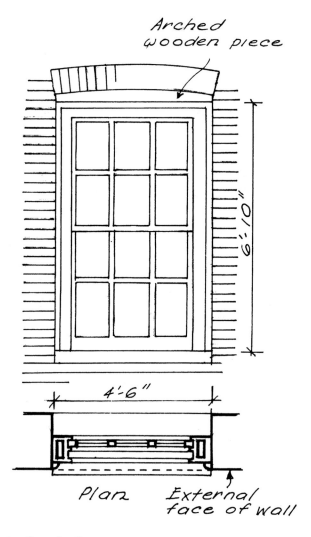

Sash windows

The sash window made its appearance in England in a limited way after the Restoration, and soon became a feature of the homes of wealthy people. It developed into the typical design feature of the Georgian house. Note that the woodwork forming part of the frame in Fig 7.18 is flush with the external face of the wall. The *Building Act* of 1709 required window frames to be set back at least 4½in

(114mm) from the wall, however, as with the *Building Act* of 1707, this regulation only applied in London. London was a large city with closely packed houses, and there was a fear of fire. With window frames set flush with the face of the external wall, flames could easily lick up and across to other areas of woodwork, for instance, to any windows above. By recessing the frame, the spread of fire was inhibited.

The increased interest in classical proportions towards the end of the seventeenth century, led to the inclusion of taller rooms in the new houses being built by people of wealth and discernment.

Until the end of the period, structural timbers and other external joinery features were built of hardwood, usually oak, which was left to weather to a silvery grey colour. Softwood, imported from Scandinavia, was a post-Restoration introduction, and it had to be painted for protection against the weather. It was used in the construction of sash windows and doors.

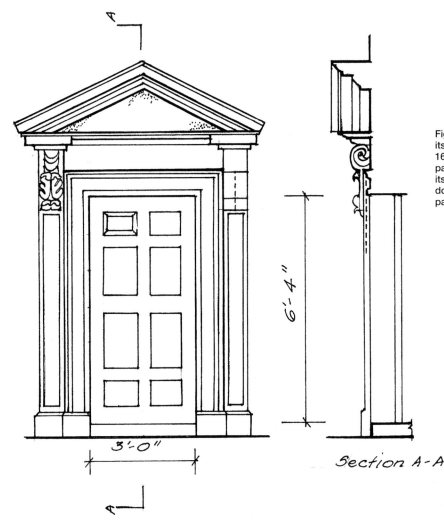

Fig 7.19 This door and doorcase, with its carved brackets, dates from about 1690 and was made from oak. The panels are chamfered, and the door itself is 2in (51mm) thick. Such oak doors and surrounds were not painted, but were treated with oil.

6'-4"

3'-0"

Section A-A

External doors

The solid, oak-planked front door already used in Tudor houses continued to be a feature in houses built throughout the seventeenth century and into the early eighteenth century in many types of homes. During the years of William and Mary's reign, oak doors in important buildings were constructed with raised panels. The ornamental carved brackets, so typical of post-Restoration Stuart times, were also made of carved oak, until the advent of the painted door and doorcase. The classical tradition of panelled and painted doorcases began to infiltrate during the reigns of William and Mary, and Queen Anne, and this type of door became popular from 1700 onwards, in large and medium-sized houses.

Panelled and painted doors were made of imported softwood and finished with lead paint. The door usually had three or six panels – sometimes even eight – and each panel was raised and had a bevelled edge. (It was quite different in appearance from the late-nineteenth-century panelled door, where the panels were recessed.)

Simulating Stuart doors

The nearest to the Stuart door in dolls' house terms, is probably an early Georgian door, of which there are several types available commercially in 1/12 scale.

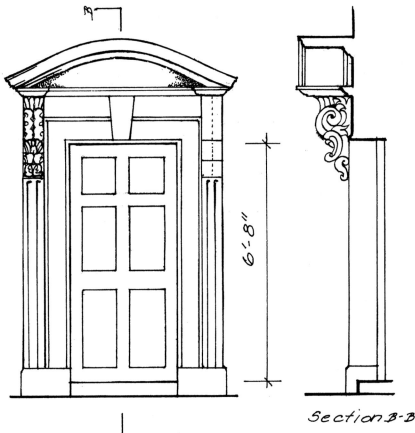

Fig 7.20 This doorway, with its canopy and brackets, dates from the late seventeenth century. It is made from imported softwood and painted white. The door panels have the chamfered edges typical of the time.

Section B-B

The door frames of these late Stuart doors were plain with square heads, and were painted to match the door. Many front doors, especially in houses built by wealthy people, were surrounded by ornamental doorcases, which were also painted. In late Stuart times, such a doorcase could be very decorative, with carved brackets supporting a projecting canopy. The canopy itself was sometimes quite elaborate, often in the shape of a semicircle, carved on the underside to represent a shell.

Fig 7.21 Doorway heads from farmhouses in the Lake District, showing carved lintels.

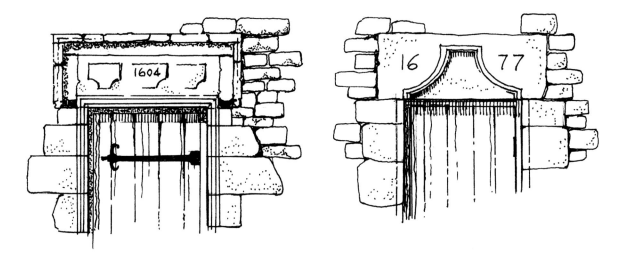

Lintels

Lintels over the early Stuart oak-planked doors were quite often carved, as they had been in Tudor times, whether they were of wood or stone. Many local characteristics can be found in these, and the north of England in particular has a tradition of carved lintels. Details of door surrounds did not vary much during the seventeenth century, but local craftsmen took the opportunity to add decoration where possible: dates were carved in lintels, and the initials of the owner were often incorporated as well.

Metalwork

The village blacksmith was kept busy making decorative hinges and other useful items, including the frames of casement windows. These were made, as in Tudor times, from iron which had been produced in forms suitable for the smith to work by hand, hence the term 'wrought iron' applied to such items.

Wrought and cast iron

Iron which had been cast in sand moulds was more brittle than that used in wrought iron work, and had only been used for making guns in previous times. Now the art of casting was being revived, and such items as firebacks and firedogs were produced. Both wrought iron and cast iron were made from ores found in the Weald

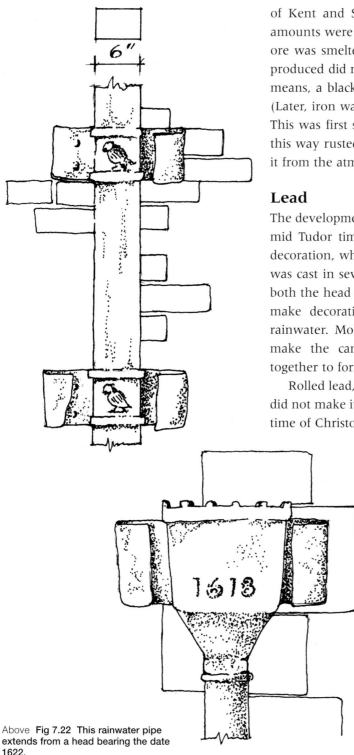

of Kent and Sussex, and in the Forest of Dean; small amounts were also present in Weardale and Furness. The ore was smelted by burning charcoal, and the iron thus produced did not rust. It corroded to produce, by natural means, a black coating of magnetic oxide for protection. (Later, iron was produced from smelting by coke or coal. This was first successfully done in 1709. Iron smelted in this way rusted and therefore needed painting to protect it from the atmosphere.)

Lead

The development of lead rainwater heads continued from mid Tudor times. They were now the subject of much decoration, which reached its peak about 1700. The lead was cast in several pieces, and soldered together to form both the head and downpipes. Cast lead was also used to make decorative cisterns, kept in gardens for storing rainwater. Molten lead was used, as in Tudor times, to make the cames which joined small pieces of glass together to form the panes in casement windows.

Rolled lead, widely used for roofing in Georgian times, did not make its appearance in the Stuart period until the time of Christopher Wren.

Above **Fig 7.22** This rainwater pipe extends from a head bearing the date 1622.

Right **Fig 7.23** A rainwater pipe and head from 1618.

Far right **Fig 7.24** This very ornate rainwater head comes from an aristocratic house.

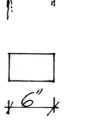

Hints on achieving Stuart effects

A

Carved wooden brackets were a feature of some Stuart (and Georgian) doorways. Buy or make a plain bracket, and stick embossed paper or lace onto it. Stuart brackets were often made from oak, so should be coloured a brownish-grey and wiped down with a tissue to imitate natural wood.

B

Decorative leadwork was another feature in Stuart times; again, use embossed paper to imitate this, and paint it a lead grey colour.

C

Semicircular or other curved doorheads can be made from papier-mâché strips over a temporary shape. This method is similar to that described for making pantiles (*see* the section on Pantiles, under Roofs in Chapter 4), using a coffee jar or other suitable glass or plastic container for the mould. Lay the jar on its side, propping it to prevent it rolling about. Smear it with Vaseline, and place one strip of lining paper on it. Apply PVA glue to the upper surface of the paper. Take another strip and lay it on the previous one, again, applying glue to its upper surface. Repeat this process three or four times, and leave to dry. Allow it to dry for a few days – do not dry it artificially. When thoroughly dry, slip the shape from the container. The front edge of the canopy can be concealed behind an ornamental shape cut from card or thin wood, and glued to it.

Chapter 8
The Georgian period

E legant crescents, long terraces and dignified detached houses of regular design, spa towns and planned cities are the pictures conjured up in people's minds when Georgian buildings are mentioned.

Historical background

The Georgian period spanned 110 years, starting with the accession of George I in 1714, and ending with the death of George IV in 1830. Because we are describing what was an ongoing historical development in terms of separate periods, we are having to use a somewhat artificial method of division – that of division by reign. Because of this, and the fact that the Georgian period is so long, it is convenient to use the further division of early and late Georgian periods when describing buildings.

The early Georgian period ran from 1714 to 1760. The late Georgian period, the longer of the two, ran from 1760 to 1830. This period takes in the Regency period, which ran from 1811 to 1820, when the old King George III died and the Prince Regent became King George IV.

Such a long period saw many changes in both political and social history, not least because of the increasing demands of an ever-growing population, which more than doubled from the start of the period to its end. At the beginning of the period, there was an estimated 5½ to 6 million people in England and Wales. During the reign of George III, this increased to 7½ million, and at the first official census in 1801, 9 million people were recorded. At the beginning of George IV's reign, the population of England and Wales was 12 million and in 1830, when he died, it was just under 14 million.

Politically, the period saw the forming of Cabinet government, of which Sir Robert Walpole was the first leading minister. It saw the Jacobite risings of 1715 and 1745 and, among other conflicts, the War of American Independence and the Napoleonic Wars.

Socially, there were developments in agriculture and industry in order to keep pace with the growing demands for food and manufactured goods from a growing population.

Developments in housing

The appearance of England changed in Georgian times. The end of the seventeenth century had seen main transport routes established, and now country villages were being connected, and cross-country routes made so that carriers could supply villagers with goods, and take produce in return. Labourers' cottages were often built along these cross routes.

The Georgian age was an age of agricultural prosperity, and owners of land were proud of their properties. They planted trees and built stables and coach houses, and some landowners built cottage homes for their farming staff. Farmers and smallholders lived in properties which were usually rented or leased, and which were sited in villages.

There were more types of domestic buildings than there had been in previous times. In descending social order these were: the mansions of the aristocracy; the fine houses of country squires; houses for the clergy; and the houses of professional men and well-to-do merchants. After these came the homes of farm staff and labourers, built by the squire on his estate, and last of all came the dwellings of the poor peasants and casual labourers, which they built themselves from materials such as thin wood and rough thatch – materials which did not last.

Agriculture

The experiments in farming methods, which had begun in the seventeenth century, now gained momentum. Viscount Townsend, with his ideas for reducing the winter slaughter of cattle by growing root crops for their winter feed, extended his realm of operations to a wide area of the English countryside. Jethro Tull introduced a seed drill, and Thomas Coke made improvements to the plough. At the beginning of the period, however, large areas of land were still farmed on the old open field system which was based on the rotation of crops. The new ideas about farming and agriculture required a different system to be implemented so, in some areas, *Enclosure Acts* were made. These often caused distress to poor people, who were forced off the land. The growth of new factory industries, using steam and water power, attracted these displaced people and resulted in the building of rows of small and cheap houses – much as it did on a larger scale in the Victorian period to follow. In many areas, cottage industries fell into a decline.

Industry

Industrial developments included those in the textile industry, the progress of steam power, and the smelting of iron ore by coke. This last had been started by Abraham Darby I in 1709. The process gave rise to the developing use of iron in construction work and the making of ornamental goods. The Iron Bridge in Coalbrookdale, built by Abraham Darby III, opened in 1781, and Thomas Telford used iron in the construction of the Menai suspension bridge in Wales, between 1819 and 1825. In the making of domestic items, both cast iron and wrought iron were used in the construction of the balconies, railings and fanlights which made such a decorative contribution to Georgian architecture.

Architecture

Architecturally, the period began with the firm appreciation of classical design as a whole, which developed through the rise of planned towns into the Age of Elegance, and ended with light-hearted buildings influenced by Indian, Chinese, Egyptian and Gothic elements.

The ownership of land in planned towns was very complex in Georgian times. It is somewhat hard to believe that the beautiful cities of Bath and Cheltenham – to use but two examples – owe their existence to speculative builders. The designs of the cities, towns and buildings therein were the responsibility of the overseeing architects. In Bath, these architects were the Woods, father and son.

Some of these graceful and well-planned towns were built at the same time as the displaced workers were being housed near factories. At least the outside frontages of town buildings looked graceful and well-designed; the backs, in some cases, left much to be desired. On the other hand, detached houses and villas, built by single, wealthy owners, showed taste and refinement on all sides, with rear windows leading onto spacious lawns.

Land values in town and city sites led to the design of the terrace house, building upwards on a narrow site, much like the town house which the Tudor merchant had developed. However, in Georgian times, it formed part of a planned entity such as a square or crescent, or a long row which looked out over lawns or wide walkways. Small terrace houses in country areas were often built in small closes or in rows overlooking village greens.

In the smaller towns, the villas where the doctor, clergyman, prosperous shopkeeper and professional man lived, also showed quiet taste. These houses had gardens which, while not on the scale of the landed gentry, made pleasant surroundings to these small homes.

Legislation

There was quite a lot of building legislation between 1700 and 1830, which affected the appearance of houses. To take one example, a *Building Act* of 1774 specified that town houses should be of four types, and that each type had to conform to certain standards of construction.

Choosing a style
Dolls' house builders have quite a range of Georgian houses to interest them, from those in a small town to those in a city. This period is quite a popular one for ready-built dolls' houses and kits, and these lend themselves to many different ways of furnishing and decorating the interior and exterior.

Plans

The development of the planned terrace in towns and cities saw the house as a unit repeated to form a pleasing composition based on classical, and therefore formal, design. This formality of design was coupled with the need for additional rooms, as the social requirements of living space for wealthier people were raised throughout the period. These social and design influences naturally affected the planned layout of the Georgian house.

While plans varied, they generally followed the symmetrical form liked by the Georgians, as is reflected in the elevations seen in Figs 8.1–8.4. Houses were either square or oblong on plan, with the frontages varying from 24–30ft (790–980mm).

Below left Fig 8.1 A terrace house of the type leased to wealthy families, and typical of the town houses which developed right through the eighteenth century. The house is built in brown brick, with flat arches of red rubbed-brick over the windows.

Below right Fig 8.2 Another terraced house of the eighteenth century. This house would have been built in a stone area, but, as with the house in Fig 8.1, the roof is of slate with a flat section covered in sheet lead. The house is built in ashlar masonry: finely-dressed limestone with fine mortar joints. The windows have shaped keystones to give stability to their flat stone arches.

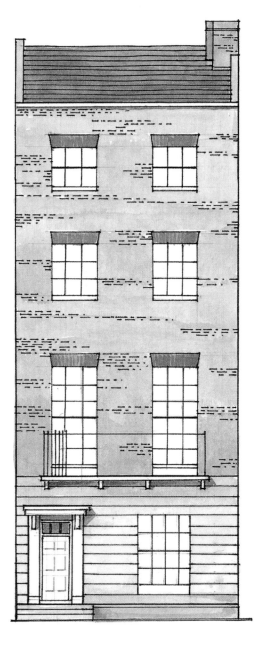

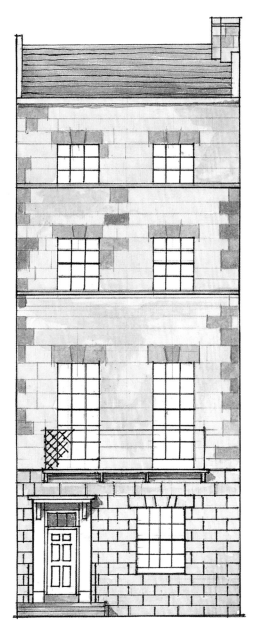

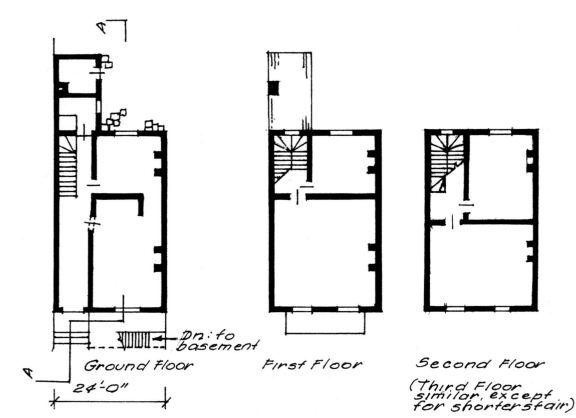

Ground Floor

24'-0"

Dn. to basement

First Floor

Second Floor

(Third Floor similar, except for shorter stair)

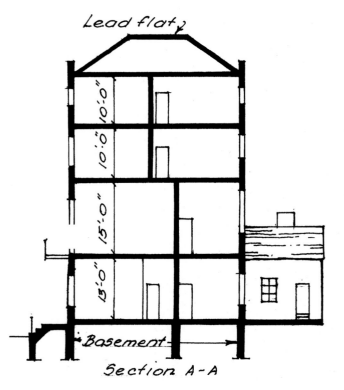

Lead flat

10'-0" 10'-0" 15'-0" 15'-0"

Basement

Section A-A

Detached houses on the outskirts of towns were also formal in design, developing gradually from the plans of late Stuart times. In small country towns, such as Lewes in Sussex and Bridport in Dorset, individual houses were sometimes built in terrace formation, in order to gain the maximum use of a narrow site. Not being planned as an entity, however, each house in the terrace was different, thus creating a street of varying character. These small terrace houses were not usually designed with basements; they were occupied by small families with few servants, and the kitchen was usually placed on the ground floor at the rear of the house.

Plans and sections of Figs 8.1 and 8.2.

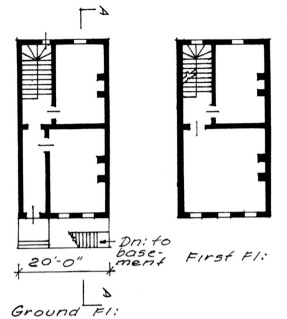

20'-0"

Ground Fl:

Dn: to base-ment

First Fl:

Second Fl:

Attic Fl:

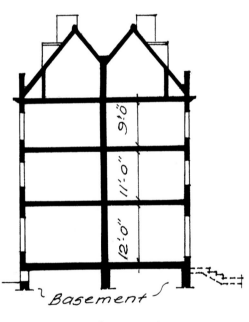

9'-0"

11'-0"

12'-0"

Basement

section A-A

Fig 8.3 A small terrace house based on a design included in *A Pattern Book for Builders.* It is built of brick, with a clay-tiled roof, and an attic storey.

Plans and section of Fig 8.3.

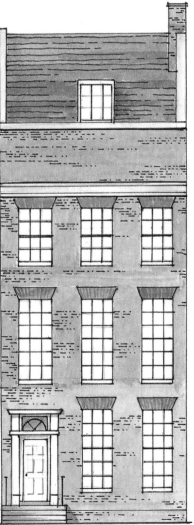

Fig 8.4 An early-nineteenth-century terrace house faced with stucco. The roof is slate.

In previous times, servants had formed part of an economic unit in the countryside; now they were often quite separated from their employer's profession or trade. In the upper classes, this separation affected house plans in the following way: ground and first floor rooms were occupied by the employer's family, be they owners or lessees; and the attics were occupied by servants. If there was a basement, this contained the kitchen, which also formed the daytime living quarters of the servants. Basements housing kitchens and store rooms were normally found in town and city houses, so that space could be given to important rooms on the ground and first floors. These basements were approached by steps leading down from the entrance area, behind railings fronting the street.

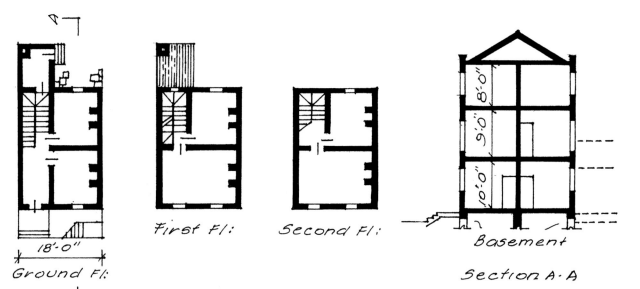

Plans and section of Fig 8.4.

Hints on adapting the plans

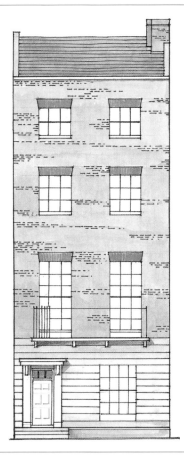
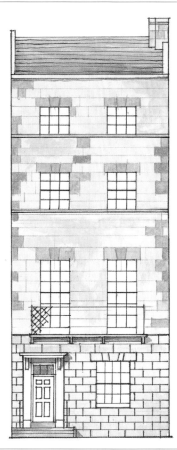

Figures 8.1 and 8.2
The front parts of the houses shown in Figs 8.1 and 8.2 can be used with a false door on the ground floor, indicating that there is a staircase beyond. Or, if you are keen on making a Georgian staircase, bring it into the front part of the house, and introduce extra walls on the first and second floors. To bring the staircase forward you will need to increase the width of the house to about 27ft (89m), or the hall will be too narrow.

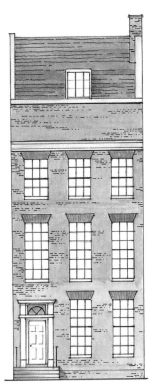
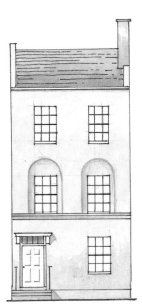

Figures 8.3 and 8.4
With the houses shown in Figs 8.3 and 8.4, use the front part or, as in the hints for those shown in Figs 8.1 and 8.2, bring the staircase forward, and increase the width of the house by about 3ft (9.8m).

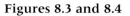

Walls

By the beginning of the Georgian period, brick and stone construction had become general for most large and medium-sized houses, especially those in towns and cities. Some small houses in rural areas continued to be built in half-timber, following the design of seventeenth century rural homes.

The use of stone or brick was dependent on the area. For example, squares and terraces in Bath and Cheltenham were built of limestone, while Weymouth mixed its Portland stone buildings with brick terraces; in south-east London, in Blackheath, brick from the local earths was dominant, but late-Georgian terraces in Truro were built of local granite.

Stone

The sophisticated stone buildings in towns and cities were built of dressed-stone blocks, with thin mortar joints, giving a smooth face to a wall. This was known as ashlar masonry. While some buildings were constructed of solid blocks of stone, bonded one into the other, the expense involved was sometimes unacceptable, so an alternative method of construction was used, whereby thinner facing slabs, still dressed, were bonded to a rough stone or brick backing with iron cramps. Small stone houses and cottages were usually built of solid blocks throughout, the cottages often constructed of undressed stone. (*See* the section on Stone Walling in Chapter 4.)

While ashlar masonry gave a smooth finish to walls, the Georgians sometimes wished to draw attention to the importance of a certain part of the building, so they emphasized the joints between the dressed stones. They did this by recessing the mortar joints and keeping the edges of the blocks square, or by chamfering their edges.

Throughout the eighteenth century, terrace houses were often leased to wealthy families. To add to the dignity of these houses, emphasis was often given to the facade of the ground floor. Figure 8.1 shows a dressed-stone facade on a brick building, with the horizontal joints of the stone recessed. Figure 8.2 shows bevelled stones on the ground floor to give a strong pattern. Houses were built of brick or stone, which could be limestone, pink or brown sandstone, or grey granite, according to the traditional materials of the area. The hardness of the stone influenced how much detail could be included.

Brick

Brickwork in Georgian times reached a high standard of crafts-manship, resulting in a pleasing, regular appearance. The Stuart period had seen the development of ornamental brickwork towards its end, and developments continued to be made, on a wide scale, in Georgian times. One such development was the use of rubbers. By adjusting the mix of clay and sand, and burning at a lower temperature, a brick softer than the usual could be produced. Such bricks were known as rubbers, and the advantage of their softness was that they could easily be cut to a specific shape, and when rubbed with another brick, they gave a smooth surface and a fine joint. Rubbers were a feature of the design and construction of Georgian window and door arches. They were a soft, bright red in colour and contrasted well with brown or grey brick walls.

The bricks used for general good quality walling were carefully made by hand, and the mortar joints were fine. The bond used was that known as Flemish.

Simulating stucco

Using a stone-coloured tint is quite an effective finish for your dolls' house, because the wooden or MDF walls can be painted with a matt-finish emulsion, and, when this is dry, the joints can be painted or pencilled in.

Imitation stone

Despite the beauty of the brickwork, there arose during this period a feeling that buildings of dressed stone were more indicative of wealth and taste than those built from brick. Attempts were made to find a substance that could be applied to brick in order to imitate stone. The year 1756 saw the introduction of such a substance, and it is believed that the Adam brothers used this material in the construction of the buildings they designed for the Adelphi in London, between 1768 and 1772. The use of a form of this cement-based paste, which was known under the general name of 'stucco', reached its peak in the early nineteenth century, when it was widely used by the architect, John Nash. Imitation joints were made by incising lines on the stucco. Because this was intended to look like stone, the surface was colour-washed a stone tint, usually cream to light buff, reminiscent of Bath limestone.

An artificial stone, called 'Coade stone' after its inventor, Eleanor Coade, came into use in the early 1770s. It was not a form of stucco, but a very durable type of terracotta, usually cream in colour. It was widely used for ornamental dressings round doors and windows set in brick walls, from the late eighteenth century through to the late nineteenth century.

Above left **Fig 8.5** An eighteenth-century brick house, typical of the detached houses built for the clergy and other professional men in small country towns.

Above right **Fig 8.6** Another detached house typical of those built for clergy and professional men. This one is from the early nineteenth century, and shows a stuccoed finish.

Simulating Coade stone

To give the effect of Coade stone decoration, the dolls' house builder can buy miniature wooden mouldings, stick these onto the face of the brick or stuccoed wall, and paint them.

Timber

The introduction of large quantities of imported softwood gave rise to the construction of timber-framed houses clad in what is known as 'weatherboarding'. These small houses form quite a feature in the villages and small towns of south-east England, especially in the Weald of Kent, and in Essex, and less frequently in other parts of the Home Counties. The weatherboarding and other joinery was usually painted white, with the newly-developed lead oxide paint. However, agricultural and small industrial buildings were usually tarred, as were some small cottages, especially those near the sea, as this protected them from the damaging action of sea salt. Farm buildings away from the sea were sometimes tarred as it was believed that the composition of the tar was distasteful to animals and thus stopped them from chewing and damaging the wood. Tar was also used in cob buildings (built from straw mixed with compacted earth) to prevent rising damp.

Wood was also used to imitate stonework, especially in the south-east. Sometimes wooden blocks were used as a cladding to imitate stones. These were often used on the corners of buildings that were hung with tiles on the fronts. This use of wooden blocks to imitate stone can look incongruous in certain circumstances, when you consider that genuine stone walls were solid and load-bearing!

Legislation

In addition to the *Building Act* of 1774, the *Building Acts* of 1707 and 1709, made in late Stuart times, also had an impact on the design of Georgian walls and roofs. (*See* the sections on Roofs and Chimneys, and Windows in Chapter 7.)

Roofs and chimneys

The considerable variation in Georgian house plans gave rise to differing roof designs.

Span and shape

The detached house, often square on plan, had four equally important elevations, the roof usually rising from behind a parapet on all four sides. The narrow-fronted terrace house sometimes showed, with its neighbour, a gable end on the street front, rising behind a parapet. This was because the roof ridge ran from front to back. Alternatively, the roof ridge ran along the terrace. (*See* Figs 8.1–8.4.) The 'Mansard' roof, introduced from France, allowed a lot of room in the attic storey. (*See* diagram e in Fig 2.6.)

Materials

Roofing materials, generally, were tiles, pantiles, stone slabs (sometimes called stone slates), slates themselves, and lead sheets. At the end of the early Georgian period, Welsh slates could be taken to different parts of the country along a network of canals. This meant that slate was now relatively easy to obtain, and cheap to transport, so slates became more common at this time. Georgian classical design required that roofs in classical buildings should not form an important design element, and slates were welcomed for this reason as well, because they could be laid to a shallow pitch of 30°, and remain unobtrusive behind parapets. Roofs were also constructed with flat areas covered with lead sheets, alongside sloping roofs covered with other materials. (*See* diagram g in Fig 2.6.)

Ridges on stone-slated roofs were covered with carved pieces of stone. The ridges on slate roofs were protected with slates placed to form a 'V' over them, or alternatively, were dressed with lead. Tiled roofs were finished with hand-made half-round tiles. (The ornamental red tiles beloved by the Victorians, were never used on any roof in Georgian times.)

Chimney stacks

Chimney stacks were very simple in medium-sized brick and stone houses. They were usually rectangular, with a simple moulded cornice.

It is believed that circular chimney pots were introduced in the time of George III – they did not project more than 2in (51mm) above the stack, so as not to be visible from the ground.

Windows

The sash window, which first made its appearance in England in the late seventeenth century, developed into the most distinctive feature of the medium-sized Georgian house. It owed its popularity to three things, one to do with design influences, and two with practical considerations.

Classical influences

The design of the sash window was such that it embodied the classical influences of the time, which favoured regularity, precision and proportion relating to the overall appearance of a building. The larger rooms that were now required in medium-sized houses had higher floor-to-ceiling heights than most of those in earlier periods, so taller windows were desired.

Softwood

From a practical, constructional point of view, the imported softwood was easier to work than the hardwood used in the casement windows of Tudor and Stuart times. This made it possible to construct moulded wooden glazing bars, set in moulded wooden frames and sashes. Because these glazing bars were rigid, as opposed to the lead cames of previous times, it was possible to use larger panes of glass, although glass was still expensive to produce. Casement windows with leaded lights were still used in small cottages.

Simulating glazing bars
Some late Georgian windows, especially Regency ones, used glazing bars made from iron or brass, and painted white, but, in full size the designs were difficult to read properly, and in 1/12 scale, the bars could be difficult to make with simple equipment. With all glazing bars, use the most practical moulding available to achieve the effect you want. There are good wooden Georgian windows with nicely proportioned panes available commercially, and these are worth looking for. Windows with curvilinear glazing bars can be obtained from specialist firms. Examples of such models can be seen in Figs 8.7 and 8.8.

Window construction

■ Because of the legislation affecting London, by which windows had to be set back from the wall face, it is easier for the dolls' house builder to build a Georgian house outside London. As altering Stuart windows to bring them up-to-date was not uncommon in Georgian times, you could do this with your dolls' house if you wished!

■ Bay and bow windows are a familiar part of the late Georgian scene, but they do offer a challenge to the dolls' house builder. The wood for the 1/12 scale bows has to be bent by soaking strips of hardwood that are moulded round a suitable shape, attaching them temporarily, but firmly, and leaving them until they are pliable. Once pliable, they must be taken out of the water, and left to dry, after which the base shape can be removed. Fortunately, 'glazing' can be carried out with acrylic sheet, which bends easily.

Far right **Fig 8.7** Typical Georgian window, with a semicircular head and curvilinear glazing bars.

Right **Fig 8.8** Square heads for windows were also popular in Georgian times.

The other practical consideration was the treatment of the softwood. Because it needed protection from the weather, it was painted with lead oxide, and it was this which gave the white finish associated with the Georgian sash window.

Size and shape

There are many theories about the proportions of Georgian sash windows, but a window was taller than it was wide as, usually, was each pane of glass, although in some less important rooms the panes sometimes reached the proportions of a square. Naturally, the size and number of the windows was relative to the size of the room which had to be lit. If there was more than one window in the same wall and on the same level, they would be identical.

A popular arrangement of the panes of glass in a medium-sized window was six panes in the upper sash and six panes in the lower. The number of panes was increased for lighting a library or salon on the principal floor, and smaller windows at the top of a house could have an uneven number of sashes – three panes in the upper sash and six panes in the lower.

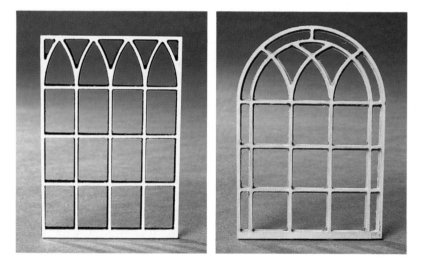

Heads

Windows lighting important rooms often had semicircular heads, and the glazing bars radiated accordingly. Square heads were also popular. The flat arch over the window was made from red rubbers. These were soft bricks, rubbed to a wedge shape and thinly jointed. They fitted tightly together and, when the mortar had set, the wedge shapes set against the key brick or keystone in the centre, prevented the arch structure from slipping.

Setting

The positioning of the sash window in the depth of the wall varied according to where and when the house was built. In London, after the *Building Act* of 1709 (passed in Stuart times), the frame had to be set back from the wall face. (*See* the section on Sash Windows, under Windows in Chapter 7.) In other places, the frame could be set flush with the outside face of the wall. A further Act relating to London was passed in 1774 – this stated that the frame also had to be recessed.

It can be confusing to date a house by looking at its windows. The Georgians were not above altering their houses to bring them up-to-date. Many a William and Mary house, occupied by a Georgian family, had its casement windows removed and sash windows inserted.

> **Window heads**
>
> For the dolls' house builder, square heads for windows are easier to construct than semicircular heads.

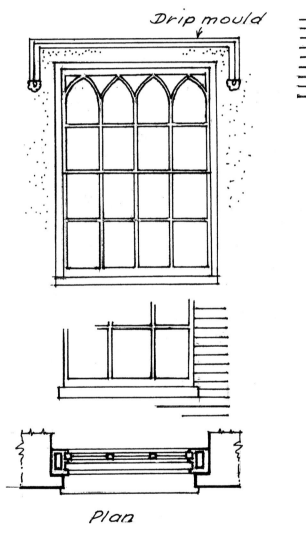

Plan

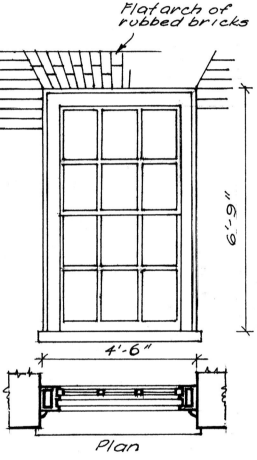

Plan

Top left **Fig 8.9** Sash window from the Regency period, set in a stuccoed wall, and with a drip mould running above it.

Above **Fig 8.10** A small, nicely proportioned sash window that is set back from the face of the wall. This was required by the *Building Act* of 1709 in London, but not elsewhere.

Above left **Fig 8.11** Plan and part elevation of a sash window, recessed in accordance with the London *Building Act* of 1774.

Bay and bow windows

A type of window that became popular in the mid to late eighteenth and the early nineteenth centuries, was the bay or bow window. The terms are often interchanged, but generally, a bay window is one that projects, whatever its shape, while the term 'bow' refers to the shape being part of an ellipse or semicircle. These windows were very popular in small villas, in seaside terraces, and in rows of small shops. You can see many examples of such windows from this period in eighteenth and early nineteenth century towns, especially in the south of England.

External doors

One of the most attractive design features of the Georgian house was its entrance doorway. Doors themselves were fairly standard in the arrangement of their raised panels, but the design of doorcases (i.e. surroundings) showed a wide variation throughout the period.

Fig 8.12 The doorway to a fairly large house in a cathedral close in the south of England. The door dates from about 1730 and is built of softwood, which has been painted.

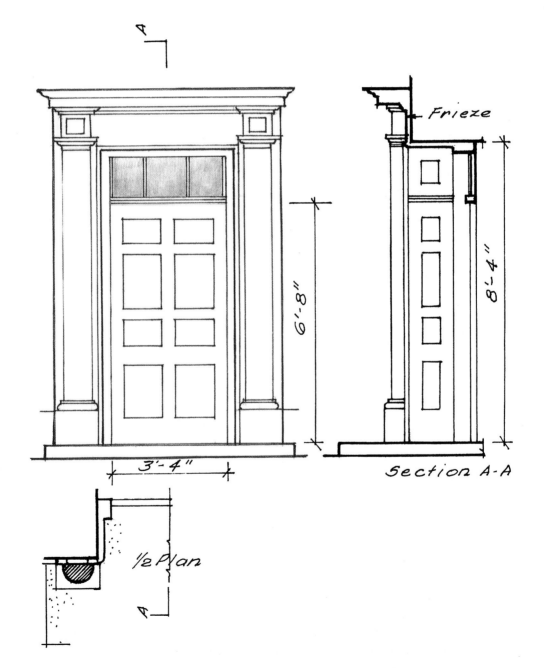

Frieze

6'-8"

8'-4"

3'-4"

Section A-A

½ Plan

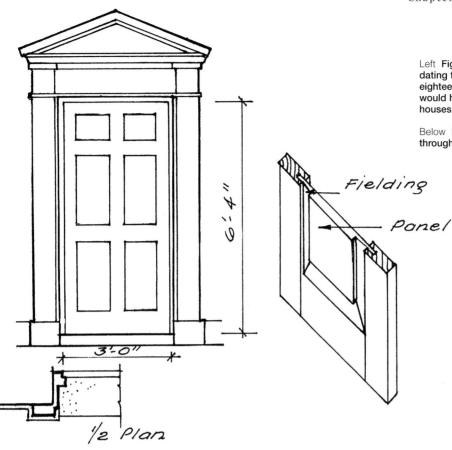

Left **Fig 8.13** A neat, simple doorway, dating from the second half of the eighteenth century. The local joiner would have made many of these for houses in small towns.

Below **Fig 8.14** Sectioned plan through a fielded panel.

Door surrounds

There was also quite a difference in the treatment of door surrounds between those in the south of England, and those in the northern upland areas. Projecting canopies and porches were a feature of some houses in the south, where they were usually made of timber, while in the north there were simple surrounds made from the local stone. In a similar way, sturdy granite houses in the south-west had plain granite porches to match. In southern counties, the easily worked softwood lent itself to the making of detailed wooden doorcases and porches in medium-sized houses, while slightly projecting hoods, supported on plain or carved brackets, were usual in small terrace houses. Mass-produced Coade stone was very popular with local builders for decorative door surrounds. They ordered their requirements from pattern books, which were the forerunners of catalogues. The decorative surround seen in Fig 8.16 is made from mass-produced items of Coade stone, including the keystone, which has a mask-like design on it. The worm-like decoration on the other stones is called vermiculation.

Fanlights

Because the plans of terrace houses, and some detached houses, had entrance halls with no windows, the fanlight above the entrance door developed. (Although properly a window, it is included in this

Door design

■ If you would like to use a colour other than white for your Georgian dolls' house door, stick to those that were available at the time, and possibly use it just for the door itself.

■ The full-size, polished hardwood door with its integral fanlight, obtainable today from joinery suppliers, is not a traditional form of door, so it is inappropriate for your dolls' house.

■ If you are buying a door to fit in your personally designed doorcase, remember that Georgian doors have raised panels while Victorian panels appear to be sunk. (*See* Figs 8.14 and 9.21.)

Fanlight design

Although the semicircle was the most popular shape for fanlights, because this is not always easy to cut out, the dolls' house builder might like to choose a rectangular design; such a design was quite usual. Models of semicircular fanlights are available commercially – one example can be seen in Fig 8.17.

section because it formed an integral part of the Georgian entrance door.) Fanlights gave scope for decorative glazing bars, made either of wood, lead or iron (*see* the section on Fanlights, under Metalwork in this chapter).

Colour

Doors, doorcases and fanlights were painted white, though the gradual development in the production of oil paint led to some colours being available at the end of the eighteenth century. These included grey, buff, fawn, various tints of pale green, olive green, dull red, pale yellow and pale orange.

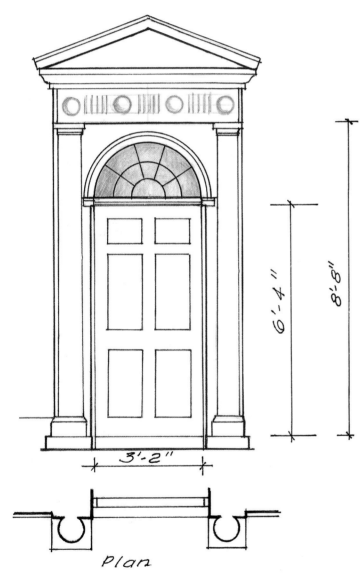

Left **Fig 8.15** A late-eighteenth-century door in London. The door, with its fanlight, is only slightly recessed from the main wall face. The whole piece is made from softwood, which has been painted. The frieze above the attached columns is lightly carved with classical motifs.

Above **Fig 8.16** This door, with Coade stone decoration, dates from between 1800 to 1810. The door and fanlight are set back from the wall face by about 6–9in (152–229mm).

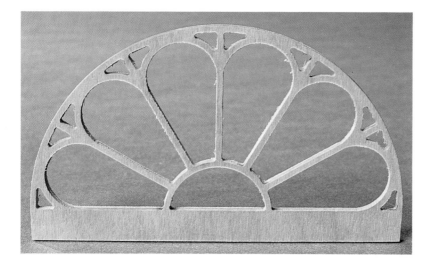

Fig 8.17 Model of a fanlight which could have been 36–48in (91.5–122mm) wide in its original setting.

Metalwork

Fencing

In previous times, the main boundaries of larger houses were delineated by walls, and post-and-rail fences. As the eighteenth century progressed, these gave way to wrought iron railings, which made a graceful contribution to the appearance of both detached houses and terraces (*see* Figs 8.18 and 8.19). Smaller houses and cottages still had low walls and fences to separate their properties from public pathways, and in some country areas, a hedge of hawthorn, honeysuckle or wild roses, made a colourful boundary.

Towards the end of the eighteenth century, and throughout the nineteenth century, cast iron was widely used for railings, as it was cheaper to produce than wrought iron for repetitive items.

Below left **Fig 8.18** London railings, dating from 1725. Typically, each upright would have been individually fixed into a continuous stone coping or kerb.

Below right **Fig 8.19** Railings in London, dating from 1810.

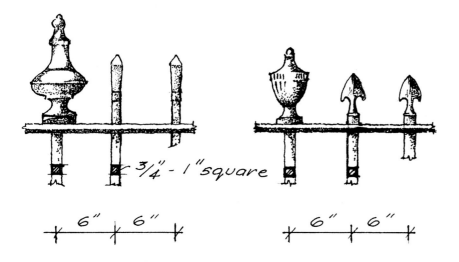

Balconies

A design feature of many Georgian houses was the balcony; a small balcony was sometimes used to emphasise a window, while some stretched all the way along a terrace. In Regency times, these balconies were often protected by shallow, sweeping roofs of rolled (sheet) lead.

Balconies were ornamental, but also served a practical purpose; windows in the principal rooms often extended to floor level, and the balcony acted as a safety barrier for people sitting or standing by the open window.

Balconies were either supported by projecting windowsills or brackets, with the ends of the balcony being tied back into the wall. Early balconies were supported by wood or stone brackets, and later ones by iron brackets. Floors of balconies were either solid, made from wooden planks spanning between the brackets, or they were made from openwork cast iron, which threw attractive shadow patterns on the wall of a house.

Fanlights

Fanlights were very decorative. The fanlights shown in Fig 8.20 could all have been made from metal, and c and d could also have been made from wood. They could be used over a simple door in its frame, or over a door with narrow pilasters at each side. Where iron was used for the frames and glazing bars, the first ones were fashioned from wrought iron, but when the demand for fanlights increased towards the end of the period, cast iron was widely used in the mass-production of popular designs.

Fig 8.20 Various fanlight designs. These particular fanlights could go over either a simple door in its frame, or one with narrow pilasters at each side.

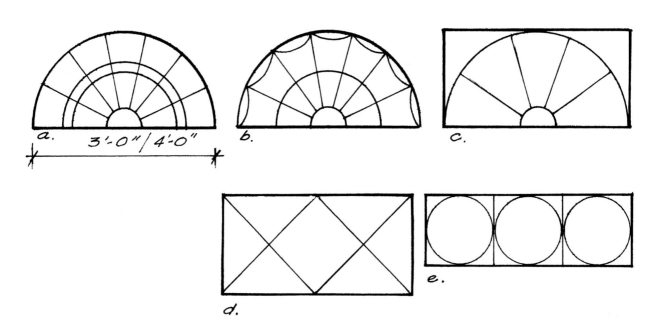

Lead

The ornamental use of lead for rainwater goods gradually died out. Where houses had parapets, the gutter was concealed behind it and, where possible, the rainwater drained to plain lead downpipes at the rear of the building. Where the classical style of building was quite severe, it was thought that ornamental rainwater heads and downpipes were unsuitable. However, smaller country houses still used decorative lead rainwater heads, as did several Regency buildings.

Preservation

Iron was now generally smelted using coal or coke. To protect the finished article from the effects of time and weather, it was painted with pitch, or a preparation made from tin. The former gave a black finish, the latter, white. (Lead oxide was also available at this time, and used to make a white paint, but this was used on wood.)

Unusual Georgian buildings

The late Georgian period saw the construction of some remarkable buildings which incorporated design elements from distant places, and also included some unusual interpretations of the English Gothic period. All of these were made in a light-hearted manner and showed a talent for adapting English and foreign styles into a happy phase of building.

One of the well-known buildings of this type is the Brighton Pavilion. It was originally built to a different design from that seen today, and was also altered internally, between 1801 and 1804, to incorporate Chinese designs – albeit an English interpretation of them. Between 1815 and 1822 it was altered externally to show the influences of the newly developed land of India with its mosques and palaces.

Another building which shows Indian influences is Sezincote in Gloucestershire, which was built around 1803 for a civil servant retired from the Indian Service.

Left **Fig 8.21 Brighton Pavilion.**

Right **Fig 8.22 The Pagoda, Kew Gardens.**

Fig 8.23 Egyptian house, Penzance.

Sir William Chambers, an architect who lived between 1726 and 1796, had travelled in China and brought Chinese design ideas back to England. Perhaps his most famous construction is the Pagoda in Kew Gardens, which was built in 1761. Another building which shows Chinese influences, though not by Chambers, is the dairy at Woburn Abbey, built around 1787.

Campaigns in Egypt during the early nineteenth century led to Egyptian designs being brought to England. There is an 'Egyptian' house in Penzance which was built around 1830 – a most unusual facade to be found in a Cornish town – and another in Plymouth, built in 1823. There used to be a building called the Egyptian Hall in Piccadilly, London, built around 1812, but this was eventually demolished.

Incorporating extra details

The unusual buildings of the Georgian period were buildings which only wealthy and somewhat eccentric people could afford. However, the small and medium-sized house often showed a small detail based on these foreign designs and on stylized English Gothic, and such details could be happily incorporated in a dolls' house. For example, a Regency window could have elaborate tracery, and a trellised porch could follow the style of Chinese Chippendale furniture which was popular at the time. Such a porch added to the front of a little two or three-storey stuccoed dolls' house could be quite charming.

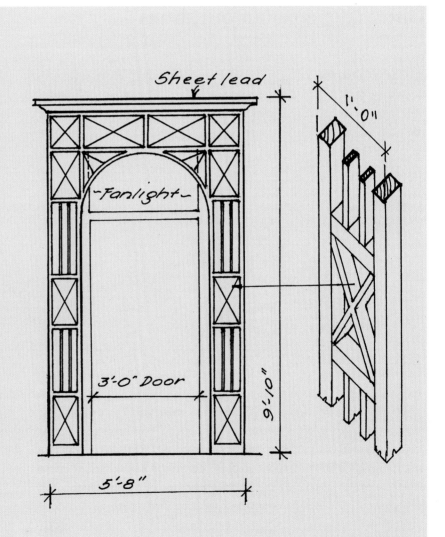

Fig 8.24 An early-nineteenth-century porch showing Chinese influences. This wooden porch could have projected about 12in (305mm), and the side panels would have used similar details to those shown in the front. Greens and reds were sometimes used to paint such a porch.

Hints on achieving Georgian effects

A

As with some Stuart doorways, carved wooden brackets were a feature of Georgian doorways. Sticking embossed paper or lace onto a plain bracket will give a carved effect: brackets can be bought or made. Georgian brackets were made from softwood, which was usually painted white.

B

For flat areas of Georgian roofs, use lead-grey paper. Sheets of lead were only available in narrow widths in Georgian times – about 24in (610mm) and were jointed by overlapping. (*See* Lead, under Building materials in Chapter 3; *see also* Fig 3.16.)

Chapter 9
The Victorian period

Much attention has been given by the press to things Victorian, in many cases highlighting the more interesting aspects of this period of diverse design. The word 'Victorian' conjures up pictures varying from the quiet homes of tradesmen, to the large villas of opulent design, housing the up-and-coming industrialists.

Historical background

The years 1837 to 1901, from the accession of Queen Victoria to her death, embrace the period of English history properly known as 'Victorian'. However, the reign of King William IV, from 1830 to 1837, really acted as an introduction to the coming years, and it is often included in the Victorian period. Perhaps it is generally seen as the harbinger of hopeful Victorian times, rather than as an anti-climax to the end of the Georgian period. King William IV spent a lot of time in his short reign tidying up and dealing with the problems of the country which his brilliant, but erratic brother had left behind. His young niece, Victoria, succeeded him to found a period of history which saw an outstanding growth of Britain and its many interests. The basis of national life at this time changed from farming to industry, and thus from rural areas to towns and cities. This, together with the influx of people from Scotland, Ireland and Europe, resulted in a general expansion of towns.

The population of England and Wales grew from just under 14 million at the beginning of the Victorian period, to 32.5 million in 1901. This rise was due to many factors, including a fall in adult mortality and a rise in fertility. Also, many Scots and Irish moved into England and Wales, and, after 1880, Jews driven from the continent of Europe, settled in London and other towns.

Developments in housing

Early in the period, it was seen that there was a pressing need to deal with the housing and other needs of the rising population; in 1861 it had already reached 20 million. Epidemics of cholera – like that of 1848 – made people realize that central bodies of authority must be responsible for levying rates and making byelaws to combat the effects of overcrowding in the rising industrial towns, which was largely responsible for poor health. It also became obvious that quicker methods of building were needed than the ways of builders and architects of previous times. The engineer now joined the builder and architect in their tasks of improving the lot of the people.

Although engineers were responsible for many large structures throughout the period, it can be suggested that their most important contribution to the life of the people was the development of the railways, with their capability of transporting industrial and building materials relatively cheaply, for long distances. Through this, machine-made bricks became available in all parts of England for use in cheap housing, and smooth Welsh slates for roofing came to the hitherto clay-tiled roofs of the south and south-east. Regional characteristics derived from the use of local materials became a little blurred, although small and remote homes far from railway stations still used local materials, and thus retained their local individualities. Also, villas in the north and north-west were still built of the local sandstone, and dignified homes in the limestone belt still used that material.

People who were responsible for industrial growth, and who employed factory workers, were able to live on the outskirts of the towns and cities, and so Victorian suburbia was born. These families lived in modest or flamboyant houses called villas. These were built in many styles, arising from the classical style of Georgian times, through a return to romantic Gothic, taking in a variety of stylized details on the way, including influences from Italy, India and Arabia. While the decoration of the Georgians had become more delicate and restrained as their period progressed, that of the Victorians became more ornate, and this was particularly evident at the time of the 1851 Exhibition.

Architecture and design

The late Victorian period saw a 'battle of the styles' between the Gothic and classical revivals (*see* Principal movements influencing architecture, on page 136). The Gothic revival had its first stirring in the late eighteenth century, when there was a leaning towards a romantic vision of the Middle Ages, and many details of that period were incorporated in buildings. The promotion of the Gothic style in later years followed a moral crusade in its use in churches and public buildings, for example, the Palace of Westminster, designed around 1835. The classical leanings of Georgian times developed into expansive classical buildings based on Greek and Italian styles. Both revivals concentrated on public buildings for their display, although details were adopted by local builders for incorporating in small houses. Some of the revival styles gave rise to opulent extravagances in details of design, which caused a reaction against them. Such a reaction can be seen in the Arts and Crafts movement, really started by William Morris, who lived from 1834 to 1896. It showed an interest in plain, craftsman-produced work, and an appreciation of decorative design elements derived from mediaeval sources. An offshoot of this movement became known as the 'Queen Anne' style. It evolved from about 1860 and became more widely used from the 1870s onwards. The name 'Queen Anne' may have arisen because the style incorporated ideas based on the domestic features of the Stuart period (*see* Principal movements influencing architecture, on page 137). A lesser influence, the Art Nouveau style, infiltrated from Europe at the end of the period. It was based on curving lines, and lent itself to the use of plant forms in decorative elements. It was to receive more attention in Edwardian times.

The seaside holiday, made popular by the aristocracy in late Georgian times due to their belief that sea bathing was good for the health, was now a popular pursuit of the middle classes who had been made wealthier by the growth of industry, and who could now travel more easily, with new rail connections between towns and the coast. Londoners went to Margate, Ramsgate, Hastings and Brighton. Other centres of attraction were Torquay and Scarborough. Such resorts usually started by being recommended by doctors as healthy places, then a developer would be found to provide streets of houses, shops and hotels – all with drainage and water supply – a promenade and some gardens. The streets of small terrace houses would be suitable for what we would now call guesthouses. (The census of 1871 shows 56 seaside towns and inland spas.)

Fig 9.1 A villa in south Devon showing classical Italianate influences, probably built between 1850 and 1860. Features include a turret and low-pitched roofs. The walls would be either finely-dressed, cream-coloured stone, or finished with painted stucco. Some corners and window surrounds have been emphasized by projecting stone or stucco work. The roofs are slated, but the turret roof is covered with glazed tiles of Italian design.

Plans

Whereas the Georgian ideal in building was based on regularity of appearance, whether in one house on its own or as a unit to form a terrace, the Victorians developed a liking for irregularity and variety in the look of their homes. The early Victorian house plan was similar to that of its late Georgian counterpart, but soon the requirements of the expanding middle classes led to a number of rooms of varying sizes and uses, the arrangement of which did not echo anything of the classical ideals of the previous Georgian period.

Fig 9.2 A north London brick villa of the Gothic revival style, built in 1869. Features include high, pointed gables with elaborate wood carving and openwork in the bargeboards, and stone settings around some of the windows. The pitch of the roof varies.

Detached houses were built showing a variety of details, including large and small windows, deep porches, steep gables and little turrets, all very decorative in their appearance.

Some of the buildings which had staircase turrets followed the Gothic revival style and thus made their turrets circular in plan, while others, built in the classic Italianate style, favoured rectangular forms. These features, together with the many variations in plan and style, are interesting to study because they give the feel of the mid- to late-Victorian home.

To return to the general plans and types of homes, pleasant terraces were still being built, some of them coming under the general name of Mansions, especially in London. These were occupied by the upper classes and the aristocracy and were built on sites with narrow frontages, as land values in cities were high. There were only two or three rooms on each floor, but the building extended upwards for four or five storeys and, in addition, possessed a basement and sometimes an attic. Smaller terrace houses were usually occupied by families of a different social standing from those in Mansions and large detached villas – social standing was very important to the Victorians. Other terrace houses included those in seaside towns, which were let out in the summer.

The *Public Health Act* of 1875 gave local authorities the power to lay down certain standards in the planning and construction of small houses. Houses built after 1875, in accordance with these standards, make up the inner suburbs of most English cities. Because land values dictated that houses be built cheaply but well, terraces were the answer. Each house had a very narrow frontage with an entrance corridor and one large front room. Another living room backed onto the front room, and upstairs were three bedrooms and a boxroom, the latter being built out over the kitchen, which was built to one side at the back and used for everyday living. Single-storey additions were built out beyond the kitchen. These housed the local authority requirements of a scullery with a copper and sink, and a separate water closet.

Victorian embellishment

The complexity of design of the Victorian period can present a daunting picture for the dolls' house builder, especially if they are constructing a house for the first time. Some houses with turrets, and many with gables, can be obtained ready-built, but not painted or otherwise decorated, from specialist firms. These give scope for personally chosen embellishments to be applied where desired, much as the Victorians did with their full-size houses. However, small houses and cottages with a simple plan, perhaps two rooms upstairs and two rooms downstairs, plus an outhouse, can be more easily constructed, either from the beginning or from a kit. These can also receive the ornamentation beloved of the later Victorians, but in a less exuberant manner than that used in larger villas.

Ornamental details are important to the feel of a late-Victorian building, and are a simple way of achieving an authentic appearance. The Figures throughout this chapter give an idea of the style of decorations used.

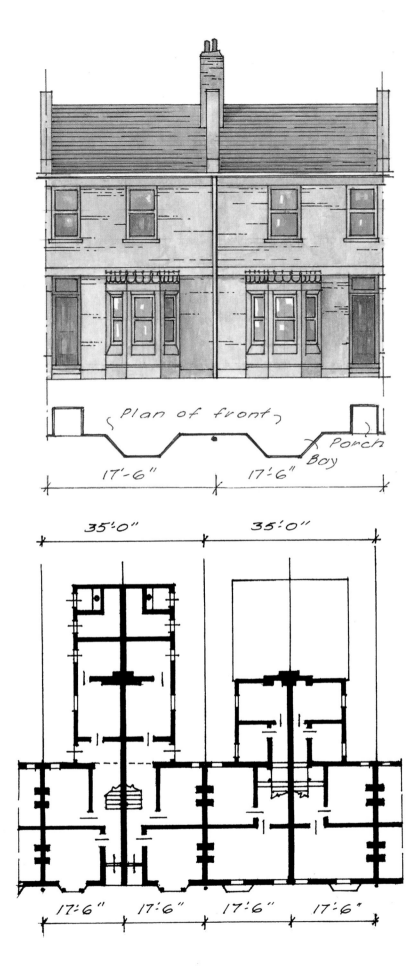

Fig 9.3 Part of a terrace of houses built in accordance with the *Public Health Act* of 1875, the plans of which were used in many English towns. The main walls are of brick, with some of the features picked out in stone or imitation stone. In some districts, walls could be faced entirely with stone. The roofs are of Welsh slate.

Plans and section of Fig 9.3.

Hints on adapting the plans

Figure 9.3

Figure 9.3 shows terrace houses and their plans. These narrow-fronted houses, with the principal rooms extending to the back and on the first two floors only, can present problems for the dolls' house builder who usually builds one room deep. Indeed, much of the social interest of the small Victorian terrace house lies in the higgledy-piggledy arrangement of its backyard buildings and small garden. By using a group of two or three houses, the front rooms alone could provide for a variety of internal finishings, including one front room furnished as a living room and another furnished as a Sunday-best room for musical evenings and visitors. On the outside, different paint schemes could be undertaken, with different front doors and porch interiors. There would also be the opportunity to introduce small front gardens with dwarf walls, fences or railings, and tiled or brick paths to the front doors. In this case, it would be necessary to use lift-off fronts for your houses, as the hinged type will interfere with your plants!

Walls

The material that made the biggest impact on the construction of walls in this period, was the machine-made brick. From the late 1850s, new methods of making bricks using machinery resulted in a cheaper product than the hand-made bricks of previous times. Transport was also easier, and therefore cheaper. Although there was an increase in the use of stone in public buildings and in large houses for the wealthy, machine-made bricks became the usual material for building houses for both the rich and poor. This was the practice even in some areas where stone was readily available, although Cornwall, Devon and the Cotswolds managed to resist any influx of the new bricks, mainly because these areas were not affected by the rising tide of large industrial developments.

Patterned brickwork

Bricks could now be made identical in size, colour and texture, which was then thought by many to be a great advantage. Also, new grinding machines could cope with the harder clays of the north Midlands and other areas of the north of England, which had not been suitable for working by hand. Previously, different coloured bricks had been made by using different clays, combined with varying local conditions of hand production. With mechanical methods, more clays were available and firing could be completely controlled, producing any colour required to a degree of uniformity. The new bricks lacked the quality of texture, but patterned brickwork using coloured bricks could be formed with precision, and the pattern showed up very clearly. Different coloured bricks could be transported to various areas, so coloured patterns could be made relatively cheaply.

Below left **Fig 9.4** Patterns made in polychrome brickwork.

Below right **Fig 9.5** Patterned brickwork, with a stone string course and keystone.

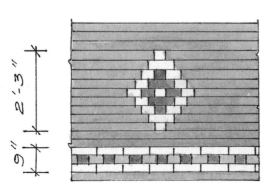

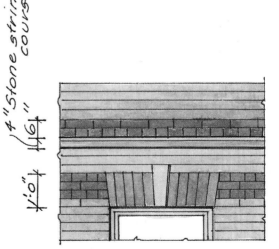

Bonding

The bond used in external load-bearing walls was that known as Flemish. It was sometimes necessary to make adaptations to the bond in order to incorporate a pattern of coloured bricks. Some late Victorian houses appear to be built in stretcher bond. This is because the load-bearing part of the wall has been built in a strong bond, such as Flemish, in cheap bricks, and a skin of good quality facing bricks has been applied to the outside, resembling stretcher bond. Bricks were also often used in conjunction with squared, roughly-dressed stone walling in small villas, where the stone was used as a thin skin covering cheaper bricks behind.

There are some buildings in London – only a few – dating from the 1880s, where early cavity wall construction has been used, and these display stretcher bond.

Decorative elements

Houses of all types used bricks to form three-dimensional design elements, such as projecting plinths and cornices. Bricks with rounded edges – called Bull-noses – were often used around window openings.

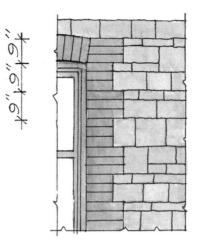

Fig 9.6 Part of a window with a brick arch and jamb, set in a wall faced with roughly-dressed stone.

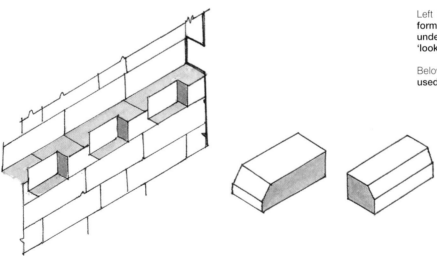

Left Fig 9.7 Projecting bricks used to form a decorative band, perhaps under the eaves. (Sketch is drawn 'looking up'.)

Below Fig 9.8 Purpose-made bricks used for plinths or surrounds.

The popularity of brickwork from the 1850s on, gradually ousted the use of stucco, which was a popular material of Regency and early Victorian times. This was not only due to the cheaper methods of making and transporting bricks, but to a desire among Victorians generally for a more lively finish than that produced by the plain and quiet surfaces of stucco. However, the fashion for stucco-fronted houses did not die out in London until the 1870s, and tall terrace houses with elaborate stucco decorations can be seen in South Kensington and Bayswater, to name but two of the areas.

Tiles

Some houses in country and suburban areas used tiles to hang on their walls. These were made very precisely from brick earths used to make roofing tiles, and were cut with one decorative end. They were used in conjunction with plain tiles to form decorative bands on a wall, or sometimes to fill a gable. Lodges and gamekeepers' cottages in country districts in the south were often decorated with tile hanging, combined with coloured brickwork and imitation half-timbering.

Coloured and patterned ceramic tiles of external quality were also used to decorate houses. They were often placed on the walls of the recessed porches of small terrace houses and larger villas, along with floor tiles. They were also used in panels to decorate the walls below and above bay windows. Panels made from terracotta or moulded brickwork were also popular.

Below **Fig 9.9** A gable wall with an ornamental bargeboard and tile-hanging. The ends of some of these tiles, which are machine-made, were cut in a pattern.

Below right **Fig 9.10** Ceramic tiles used to form a panel, which has been set in a stucco surround beneath a bay window. This example is from Weymouth.

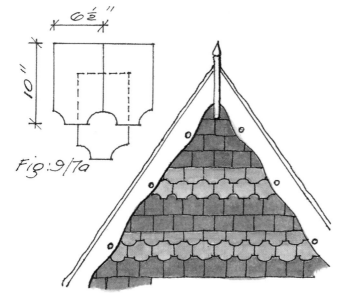

Terracotta

Another material widely used for the decorative features beloved by the Victorians was terracotta. This was made from mixtures of very fine sands and clays to produce various colours. Water was added to give plasticity, and the wet mixture placed in a mould, and then fired under controlled conditions. In days gone by, terracotta had been used in external plaques in the Tudor buildings at Hampton Court, using the techniques brought over by European craftsmen. In Victorian times, terracotta was often produced in large slabs – usually red or cream-coloured – and used for facing buildings like shops, public houses and museums. These slabs were finished with a light glaze.

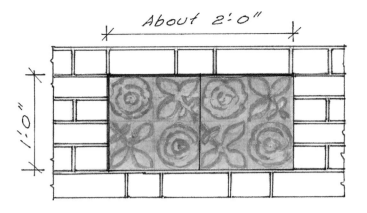

Fig 9.11 Terracotta panel set in a brick wall. These panels were often used, as here, beneath a window.

Coade stone

Coade stone was used for decorative features made using moulds (*see* the section on Walls in Chapter 8). With the emphasis on applied decoration, Coade stone, and its imitators, was very popular. Once a mould had been made, the item could be reproduced in great numbers, and the builders of the time could buy all types of ornament 'off-the-peg'.

Roofs and chimneys

The complex plan of the villa in late Victorian times led to the asymmetrical form of its outward appearance. It follows that the design of the roof was also complex. (*See* the section on Plans in this chapter.) Roofs covering small houses or terraces were simpler in form, reflecting simpler plans.

Decoration

Decorative features of the later Victorian home, whether the large villa or the smaller house, included ornamental ridge tiles and fretted bargeboards for gable ends. Roofs over bay windows were either pitched or flat. Where they were flat and lead-covered, they were finished with either a low stone balustrade or an ornamental cast iron edging.

Fig 9.12 Ornamental ridge tiles made from brick earths. These were usually red in colour, and ranged between 12 and 24in (305 and 610mm) in length. They were widely used on grey slate roofs.

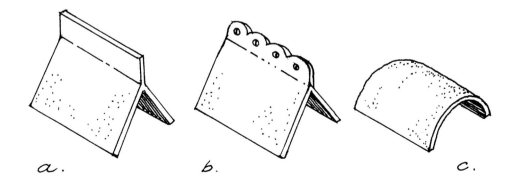

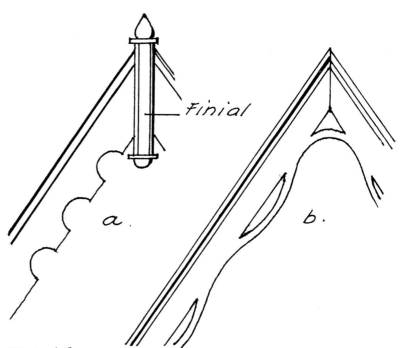

Fig 9.13 Bargeboards with fretted (cut-out) decoration. Sketch also shows a timber finial as a junction between the sloping boards.

Materials

The materials which covered the early Victorian roofs continued to be used in the late Georgian way of building, and this was carried on in many small rural homes throughout the nineteenth century. However, the villas and terrace houses of the mid- to late-Victorian times – and other smaller houses on the edges of towns – took advantage of cheaper transport, to use Welsh slates on pitched roofs. Rolled sheet lead was still used on spires, domes and flat areas as it had been in Georgian times. Copper was sometimes used on domes and turrets; it weathers to a light blue-green.

Chimneys

Chimney pots were a delight to the late Victorians, as they gave added variation to the roof line. Because of the number of fireplaces

Fig 9.14 Earthenware chimney pots. Sketches a and b are cylindrical, and sketch c is square on plan.

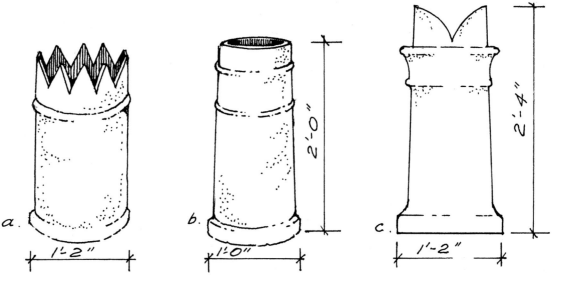

which used solid fuel in the form of cheap coal, flues were given extra height with tall chimney pots, to reduce downdraughts which caused fires to smoke. These were usually made of earthenware in a red or buff colour, were any size up to just over 12in (305mm) across, and of varied length, to project above the stack itself.

Windows

The sash window, a legacy of Georgian times, was the most favoured choice of the Victorians. However, it changed its appearance from 1838, when cheap glass became readily available through a different method of production, which yielded large panes. These large panes of glass were set in the frames of the sashes without the strengthening effects of the many horizontal and vertical glazing bars which were typical of the Georgian window. In some cases this caused some stresses in the sash joints. It was thought that these stresses could be overcome by extending the side pieces of the frames (the stiles) downwards so as to form a downstand (a 'horn') in each side piece, thus giving more timber to form a mortice and tenon joint. This was also cheaper to construct than the double dovetail of the Georgian window. An additional practical advantage was that the horns stopped the top sash from coming right down onto the sill, and trapping an unwary hand.

Below left **Fig 9.15** A small sash window with a stone lintel, set in a brick wall.

Below right **Fig 9.16** A small sash window in a stucco surround.

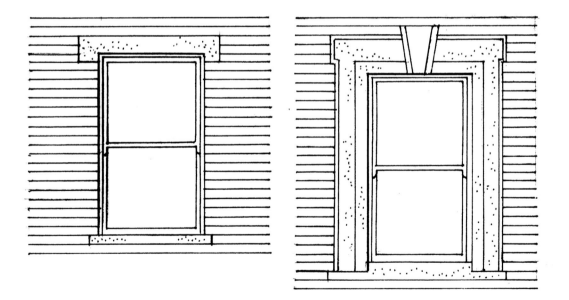

The sashes of the Victorian window were sometimes glazed with a single pane, or subdivided, with wooden glazing bars, into two or four sections. There was a variety of glazing patterns in the Queen Anne revival style, where mixtures of large and small panes were often used in sash windows. This style also used casement windows with different arrangements of glazing bars. Decorative casement windows were also used in Gothic revival houses, and in cottages built on country estates, following the Picturesque style. (*See* Chapter 10; *see also* Principal movements influencing architecture, on page 137.) The ordinary small cottage used the simple and plain casement, usually subdivided by a horizontal wooden glazing bar, thus fixing two panes of glass.

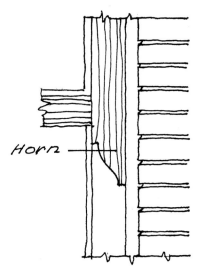

Fig 9.17 Detail of 'horn' from a sash window.

Fig 9.18 Alternative designs for sash windows.

Fig 9.19 Gothic-style, wooden casement windows, set in a stone surround within a brick wall. The building also has stone corners. This style was favoured for vicarages, halls and similar buildings in the south of England.

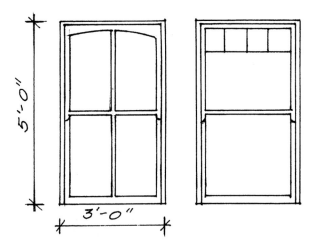

Bay windows

The bay window was the result of builders seeing that the outlook of living rooms could be improved by the installation of a window giving three aspects. Sunlight could also be appreciated at different hours of the day. Having welcomed the uninterrupted views made possible by the use of large panes of glass, the Victorians then hung lace curtains to stop light coming in and fading wallpaper and furnishings, thus lessening the visual advantages gained!

Stained glass

The art of making stained glass enjoyed a revival after 1840, when it was produced mainly for church windows. By 1870, however, forms of stained glass were made for domestic buildings. These were sometimes combined with frosting and etching to give obscurity with translucency. Coloured, obscured glass was widely used in hall and staircase windows, thus giving light, while maintaining the privacy of the people inside. In a lot of cases, it also served to block out the unsightly walls of buildings nearby.

External doors

The front doors of the early Victorian period, directly following the end of the Georgian, still echoed the designs of that time. As the Victorian period progressed, however, a typical design developed that was used in the front doors of small houses; this consisted of four panels, the longer ones being in the upper part of the door. The main difference between the Victorian panels and those of the preceding period, was that Victorian panels were flat and recessed, whereas Georgian ones were chamfered and raised. (*See* Figs 8.14 and 9.21.)

Simulating stained glass

The effect of stained glass can be achieved quite easily. The dolls' house builder can buy transparent peel-off sheets of coloured designs, which can be cut up and stuck onto firm acrylic sheet, to make decorative window and door panels. Alternatively, plain acrylic sheet can be coloured with felt-tip pens.

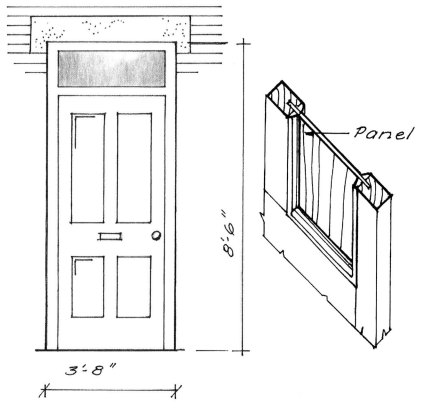

Far left Fig 9.20 A simple door for use in a cottage or small terrace, especially in those facing directly onto a public street. (Glass, indicated by shading, would have been coloured or engraved.)

Left Fig 9.21 Detail of a recessed wooden panel, used in doors of this period. (Compare the Georgian fielded panel in Fig 8.14.)

Right **Fig 9.22** The grand door of a larger villa, which would have had a front garden extending around the sides. The door would be protected by a porch, either recessed or built onto the front of the house to make a grand feature.

Far right **Fig 9.23** This door would have been used for a small house with a front garden, and would be set back within a built-in porch.

(Glass, indicated by shading, would have been coloured or engraved.)

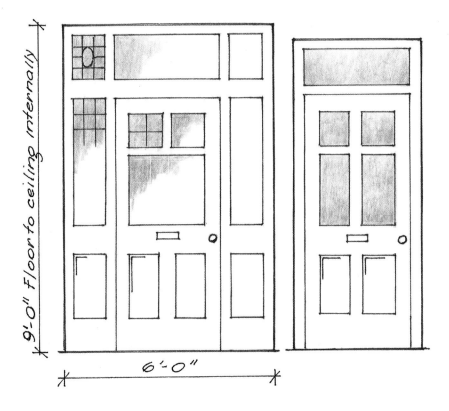

Decoration

This basic design of the front door developed into a more elaborate one that later Victorians used to impress their visitors waiting for admittance. Door furniture was made from either brass, for the wealthier homes, or cast iron.

With the production of cheap, strong glass, it was now possible to incorporate large panes in the door itself, thus replacing some of the solid wood panels. This new glass was capable of being engraved or made into decorative, coloured panels, thus giving light to the interior hallway, while maintaining privacy.

Porches

Decorative doors were often combined with porches, which were either added to the front of a house or recessed behind the front wall. Recessed porches gave great scope for decoration: panels of moulded and glazed coloured tiles were often set in the side walls, and the floor area was often laid with matt-finished encaustic tiles in black and white squares, with brown borders. Doors set back within a built-in porch were often used in the houses built after the *Public Health Act* of 1875.

External porches in grand late-Victorian houses either followed the classic or Gothic revival styles, and were built of stone or brick and stucco. Many porches were constructed with turned wooden uprights and other features in the Queen Anne revival style (*see* Principal movements influencing architecture, on page 137).

Metalwork

Although wrought iron was used for specific purposes, it was the Victorians' love of cast iron that made itself felt in decoration throughout the period.

Cast iron

As its name suggests, cast iron was produced by pouring molten iron into sand moulds (casting), where it was left to cool and set. This meant that identical items could be produced in large quantities. Ornamental cast iron was used in the production of street railings, balconies, crests (often used on roofs over bay windows), finials, rainwater heads and downpipes, and door furniture – all for the embellishment of houses. Wealthier houses usually had brass rather than cast iron door furniture.

Railings

From the 1850s, street railings were frequently round in section and sometimes twisted in a barley-sugar twist. During this period, castings were quite elaborate, with scrolls and foliage designs.

General

Cast iron was also used for more down-to-earth products like coal-hole covers, which usually incorporated the name of the iron manufacturer as an advertisement. Galvanized iron in sheet form was used for making cowls for chimney pots, and for some rainwater goods.

External paintwork

Victorian oil paint was generally made from linseed oil and white lead (lead oxide), coloured with powdered pigments. Factories for the production of lead oxide were established along the Thames estuary in Georgian times. As the nineteenth century progressed, manufacturers started to produce ready-mixed, coloured oil paints.

Colour

Coloured oil paints were used to decorate woodwork. The white paint was sometimes tinted with the addition of a little lamp-black to produce a silver-grey, or a small quantity of yellow ochre to make a creamy-yellow colour. Because the exteriors of buildings in towns soon got dirty due to smoke and other industrial pollution, dark colours were developed and used. The range of available colours was very limited compared with that used today. Typical Victorian colours used on the outside of windows and doors were black, grey, creamy-yellow, dark reds (maroon shades), browns, and a wide range of greens.

Metalwork designs
To get an idea of railings and other metalwork designs of the time, it is useful for the dolls' house builder to look through reproductions of Victorian catalogues.

Colour schemes
For a dolls' house, green paint looks well against reddish brickwork, and brown paint is effective against cream or golden stonework.

119

Finishes

A paint finish popular for the decoration of front doors was that known as graining, in which cheap wood was painted to imitate expensive hardwood. Where external walls were finished with stucco, they were painted in a cream or light buff, similar in colour to a creamy limestone.

Black-and-white houses

It is believed that the Victorians were responsible for the appearance of the black-and-white colour of the half-timbered houses of the west and north-west of England. Before the nineteenth century, the timbers must have been left to weather naturally. It is not clear why these particular areas received the black-and-white treatment, while houses in the south were left alone, though one theory suggests that houses in the wetter climate of the west and north-west needed the additional protection of oil paint. (If this was the case, one wonders why pitch or tar had not been used earlier.)

Railings

The Victorians developed cast iron into exuberant forms of decoration, including railings to front their properties. These were usually painted black, but in some cases, where the owner was interested in the classical style, they were painted to look like weathered bronze. The Victorians realized that original Greek or Roman metalwork would have been made in bronze, and as they could not afford real bronze railings, they painted them a blue-green, which is the colour to which bronze weathers, rather as copper does.

Painting railings

If the details of blue-green railings are picked out in gold, the effect on the front of the dolls' house is quite attractive.

Hints on achieving Victorian effects

A

The wide use of Coade stone, terracotta and moulded brickwork with their various shapes can be replicated using self-hardening clay, Fimo or other similar modelling compounds.

B

The Victorians' love of cast iron manifested itself in many ways, including elaborate balconies and crests, and ornate railings. To interpret these, buy some rich-looking border lace in black or white, and stick it onto clear, sturdy acrylic sheet.

C

For plain railings, the Victorians used uprights that were sometimes circular in section, and sometimes square. For the circular railings, wooden cocktail sticks are useful. They can be inserted into strips of wood, top and bottom. The bottom strip should be glued to the kerb or parapet and painted to match, so that it looks as if the upright is inserted directly into the kerb. Ornamental heads can be made from one of the modelling clays.

D

Rainwater pipes can be made from rectangular mouldings or dowelling, and their ears from thin card. Cast iron rainwater heads can be made from pieces of flat wood thick enough for the rainwater downpipe to fit under. These heads can be decorated with embossed paper, and painted.

Chapter 10
Small cottages

I t is interesting to think that the buildings we now call cottages were, from about the sixteenth century onwards, the homes of well-to-do people. The true cottage – the home of the 'cottar' or poor peasant – was built of such flimsy materials that it has long since perished.

I will use the term 'cottage' as we consider it today; a small, relatively comfortable country or town dwelling with enough space to give scope for old-fashioned furnishings, cooking arrangements and sleeping areas.

Plans

Cottage plans differ widely according to region and period. Before the sixteenth century, a cottage might have two rooms on the ground floor, with a through passage from front to back. One room, used as a kitchen/living room, would be open to the roof rafters and have a central fire – just like the larger hall houses of the time. The other room would be used for storage, and have a ladder leading up to a sleeping area above. By the middle of the sixteenth century, there would be a stone or brick fireplace at the side of the hall, with a simple staircase either winding round the back of the chimney breast, or consisting of a straight flight leading up to the sleeping area above.

Fig 10.1 A Cornish cottage, built of granite and slate and partly white-washed. The porch is a sturdy affair, providing protection from gales. (There is a parallel in porches of small cottages in parts of the Lake District.)

As I have mentioned elsewhere in this book, small dwellings, especially in rural areas, did not change very much in their outward appearance throughout the seventeenth, eighteenth and early nineteenth centuries, although generally, their plans developed according to local or national social conditions. As the seventeenth century progressed, cottages would have two or three downstairs rooms with ceilings, with sleeping places in the roof spaces. Cottages of the late eighteenth and nineteenth centuries had ceilings both downstairs and in the bedrooms above. However, many poor people still lived in cottages with few rooms, and slept in a loft which was reached by a ladder.

Fig 10.2 A particular way of building brick chimneys developed in the south of England after bricks became plentiful and affordable. To deal with the diminishing size of the stack, the bricks were 'tumbled-in'. This technique was also used on gable ends. The cottage has a brick ground floor, a tile-hung upper storey, and a tiled roof.

In rural areas, terraces of cottages usually date from the late eighteenth century. They were constructed from local materials and built by local landowners for local workpeople. It was a different story in the expanding towns during the mid to late nineteenth century where cheap, small terrace houses were built for families who had come in from the depressed agricultural regions looking for work in the growing factories.

Fig 10.3 A late-eighteenth to early-nineteenth-century weaver's house in west Yorkshire, with long, continuous windows inserted to light the workrooms. It is built of a dark, hard Pennine stone with a stone-slabbed roof.

Fig 10.4 This cottage is partly built of red sandstone from around the Brendon Hills in Somerset. The bakehouse chimney and oven are of a type often seen in the south-west of England. It was built in a circular form because the small pieces used in its construction did not form good corners.

External appearance

In some areas, social conditions did make a significant difference to the external appearance of a cottage. For instance, in those areas where weaving was carried out as a cottage industry, the first floor would be taken up with the installation of hand looms, and the room would be lit by a range of mullioned windows. (*See* Fig 10.3.) In the south-west particularly, a feature was made of an external chimney stack which served as a separate bread oven. (*See* Fig 10.4.)

Cottages also showed details that were not always used in larger houses: differences in windows and porches arose due to such things as variations in climate, and chimneys varied in shape and form according to the materials available. Figures 10.1–10.4, and Fig 10.8 illustrate some of these details.

Internal features

The most important feature of a cottage was the kitchen/living room fireplace, which dealt with the need for warmth and provided a means of cooking. Before the advent of the kitchen range in the 1780s, cooking was done directly over the kitchen fire, by means of suspended cooking pots.

Early cottages had floors of beaten earth, or a mixture of lime, coal ash and clay dust. It was not until later that the better cottages were floored with brick paving, flagstones or timber planking, the latter usually elm.

As a general rule, and according to the wealth of the original builder, a cottage could be built with one, one and a half or two storeys, sometimes with an additional room in the roof. Room heights were low compared with those in small houses built today; people were generally smaller in those times, and the ceiling height of main rooms could be as low as 6ft 9in (206cm).

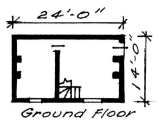

24'-0"

14'-0"

Ground Floor

Upper Floor

Fig 10.5 A late-seventeenth-century cottage built of Cotswold limestone. The entrance on the gable end is characteristic of Cotswold cottages built at this time.

Plans of Fig 10.5.

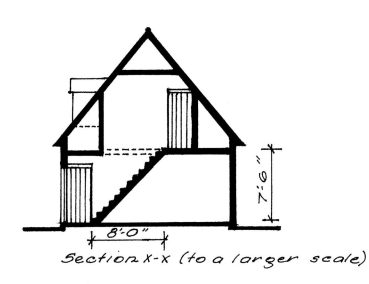

Fig 10.6 A Warwickshire cottage with quite heavy structural timbers. It would originally have had wattle and daub infill panels, but, from the late seventeenth century onwards, these were replaced by brick as they decayed. The roof tiles would be made from the same brick earths, and probably replaced earlier thatch.

Plans and section of Fig 10.6.

7'-6"

8'-0"

Section X-X (to a larger scale)

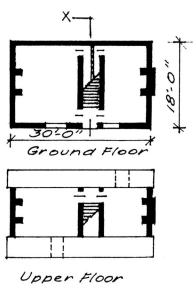

X

18'-0"

30'-0"

Ground Floor

Upper Floor

X

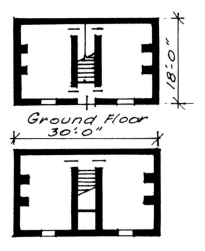

Ground Floor
30'0"

18'0"

First Floor

Fig 10.7 This house, from the north of England, probably dates from the nineteenth century. It is built of hard stone, which has been whitewashed. The roof is covered with pantiles. This type of plan, with various outbuildings (not shown), was widely used throughout England.

Above right **Plans of Fig 10.7.**

Slates

Slates

Fig 10.8 Chimney from a Lake District cottage. It was built from small pieces of local quarry waste for reasons of economy, and in a circular form because the small pieces would not form good corners. Thin pieces of slate were inserted to throw off the heavy rainfall of that area.

Model villages

During the eighteenth and nineteenth centuries, some landowners built model villages on their estates in the Picturesque style. Such cottages were built as part of a designed layout. Examples can be seen at Milton Abbas in Dorset, started in 1773; Blaise Hamlet near Bristol, built between 1810 and 1812; and Selworthy, which used Blaise Hamlet as a model, but was built in the traditional cob and thatch of Somerset. The sad thing about these 'villages' was that they were not a genuine reflection of village life, but followed an idealized view of the rustic charm of the old cottages dotted about the countryside which were, in reality, inhabited by poor families, struggling for a basic existence.

The 'villages' mentioned above were in agricultural areas. There were also philanthropic landowners who built communities for their industrial workpeople. Sir Titus Salt built Saltaire which was finished in the mid 1860s. Quaker factory owners also built good housing, as did some of the railway companies.

Hints on developing a plan

A

Descriptions of small cottages can often be found in historical novels, especially where those descriptions cover the trades of copper, tin and coal mining, fishing, farming, and weaving. It could be quite interesting to take such a description from a favourite book, look up a few more social and historical facts about the place, and build a cottage from this information. (Of course, this line of action could apply to any size of house, not only cottages, and could include upper class and aristocratic homes.)

B

Simple cottages which could easily be adapted for dolls' houses are shown in the sketches and plans of Figs 10.5–10.7. The plan with a central stair, flanked by a room either side as can be seen in Fig 10.7, is particularly suited for this. Most cottages were built with outhouses attached (not shown on plan), usually approached from the kitchen/living room. These outhouses contained a sink, and a copper, along with other basic equipment. If there was no piped water supply (*see* Chapter 11), there was sometimes a pump near the back door.

C

If you are building your cottage from the beginning, it is advisable to first work out the space which will be occupied by the staircase. A typical staircase, drawn to a larger scale, can be seen in section x–x of Fig 10.6. This example uses risers of 7in (178mm) and treads of 8in (203mm). These dimensions cope with a floor-to-floor height of just under 90in (229cm) with 13 risers, and a floor space of 8ft (244cm) with 12 treads. Cottage stairs were very steep and could rise at an angle of 45°, with treads of the same size. If you buy a ready-made flight of stairs, it will probably be at an angle of 45°, and you can cut it to fit the floor height you wish.

D

The dolls' house builder interested in constructing a cottage, either from the beginning or from a kit, would be well advised to study some examples of cottage life in local museums. Many small museums, as well as the larger ones, can be rewarding in this field, and the inside of a small cottage – perhaps with its nineteenth century inhabitants – can be very interesting to reproduce.

Hints on construction

A Figs 10.9–10.11 show three views of a two-roomed cottage which I designed and built myself, really just to find out what could be done in a simple way with no special tools, but lots of enthusiasm! I propose to grow some greenery up the walls and perhaps onto the roof, but that is still to come. The cottage is quite simple in design; it is not based on a particular style, but shows some characteristics of Kentish building, with its half-timbered front and tiled roof.

B The methods and materials I used to build the cottage may help with constructing your cottage. It is made from plywood, with a lift-off front, and measures 21 x 11in (533 x 280mm) on plan. It is divided into two rooms, with a back door in the kitchen/living room, which would have led into a scullery with a sink and water pump. Water was also collected from the roof into a rainwater butt. Although it was built earlier, I envisage this little cottage as being occupied around 1890, by a neat little widowed elderly lady, who enjoys looking after her small garden – hence the basket of vegetables on the doorstep.

C The rooms are divided by a large rough-plastered fireplace, for which I used Tetrion on a base of balsa wood blocks. This fireplace houses a cottage range which serves for cooking and heating. The ceilings are oak-beamed and stained. I used balsa wood for the beams, because the irregularity of the grain gave a realistic appearance. The floor of the kitchen imitates grey paving brick, made using commercial bonded sheets of grey brickwork, in stretcher bond, and the bedroom has a stained floor made of timber planks (probably elm in real life), imitated by inscribing lines on plywood.

D Lighting is by means of candles, and sanitation is coped with by an outside earth closet, a detail of which is shown in Fig 11.1.

E Furnishings are simple and reflect cottage life, especially the rocking chair, spinning wheel and patchwork quilt.

Fig 10.9 Model cottage with its half-
timbered front in place.

Fig 10.10 The lift-off front can be
removed to display the interior.

Fig 10.11 The oak-beamed ceiling.

Chapter 11 Drainage and sanitation

It might seem rather removed from the subject of dolls' houses to talk about drainage and sanitation, but people sometimes wonder what sort of arrangements existed in past times, and how they affected the layout of houses. If you have, or are building, a period house occupied by period people, then the arrangements for washing and other sanitary facilities – or the lack of them – would be one of the internal features of the building. Such features also had an effect on the exterior of houses in some cases, for example, external waste pipes and outside earth closets in rural areas, so the dates for the appearance of these is of interest.

As a background, here is a very brief history of drainage and sanitation, including water supply, through the ages.

Roman Britain

It is a far cry from the baths and flushing latrines of Knossos and ancient Egypt to the close-stools of seventeenth and eighteenth century England, but there is a connection, under the name of hygiene, although this was not always apparent in heavily populated and closely built towns.

The Romans knew all about the benefits of bathing, and they built luxurious bathing places, which doubled as social meeting areas. Roman villas in Britain possessed baths on a domestic scale.

The Roman occupation of Britain lasted from 55 B.C. to 410 A.D. When the Romans left, the invading forces of Saxons, Danes and Jutes plundered the Roman buildings and let them fall into disrepair. Many facets of the civilized domesticity of the Romans disappeared, including the art of plumbing. Fortunately, there are Roman remains at Bath, York, St. Albans and other places, which indicate what domestic life was like in Roman times.

Post-Roman Britain to Middle Ages

The post-Roman pioneers of water supply and drainage were the monasteries. There is a twelfth-century map of Canterbury Cathedral which shows a water supply and drainage system which was most efficient. There was a bathhouse, latrines and privies, the two latter known as 'necessary houses'. In all monasteries, there was a 'laver' or 'lavatorium' near the refectory for the monks to wash their hands; this was not a polite euphemism, it really meant 'to wash' – the term 'lavatory' is misused nowadays to mean a watercloset (WC).

Towns in the Middle Ages drew their drinking supply from wells or springs. In 1237, London drew its piped water from springs at Marylebone, by means of lead pipes. Some water mains in London and elsewhere were made from hollowed out elm trunks, elm being very resistant to the action of water. These trunks were used just as they came from the fellers, without even removing the bark.

All over the country garderobes were built on the outside of large houses; these were turrets through which human waste was discharged from a recess inside the building directly into a moat or watercourse below. For those living in small cottages and hovels, waste was usually dug into the land.

The sixteenth to eighteenth centuries

In 1582, a water wheel was built in one of the arches of Old London Bridge to work a pump that carried river water to houses in the city. This water was not clean enough for drinking, but was useful for washing and cleaning.

In the early seventeenth century, Sir Hugh Myddleton created a New River which was an open channel carrying water for bathing, clothes washing, and the 'disposal of rubbish' – where to is not clear. Even so, the New River was cleaner than the Thames, for by now, that river was taking all human dirt and rubbish.

In the sixteenth, seventeenth and eighteenth centuries, the close-stool took the place of the garderobe of the Middle Ages. This was a movable piece of furniture, unhygienically upholstered, which contained a pot. It was, of course, the duty of the servants to remove the contents of the pot. In Edinburgh, during Queen Anne's reign, it was the practice every morning, to throw the contents of the close-stools out of the windows of the tall buildings, which could be up to 10 storeys high, with a warning cry of 'gardy-loo', (Gardez-l'eau) to the people below. The city authorities eventually cleared the mess away. Hogarth described a similar scene in London some 30 years after Queen Anne's time.

Of course, these unhygienic arrangements gave rise to disease and fatal illnesses in many areas, due to the rising population and the close proximity of town buildings. In sparsely populated rural areas, people dug their waste lightly into the topsoil of their fields, much as organic farming is carried out with animal waste today. Many of those rural areas escaped the disease which was rife in towns and cities, but where water was supplied by wells or streams, as opposed to springs, these often became polluted, and were the cause of epidemics right into the twentieth century.

In Georgian times, many middle and upper class families installed waterclosets in their town houses. Records in London show some houses having them as early as 1733, with more built in the 1770's and 1780s. The waste from these waterclosets inside the houses (and from privies outside), drained into cesspools, most of which had no outlet into a main drain. They thus had to be emptied periodically by hand and pail, and the contents had to be carried away in a cart, usually by night.

The nineteenth century

The watercloset, in its various forms, developed through Victorian times and became an integral part of medium-sized houses. It took a long time for the principles of drainage without escaping sewer gases, to be understood, but eventually satisfactory schemes evolved – satisfactory that is, in relation to the immediate vicinity of a building. Unfortunately, the provision of WCs, while coping with the immediate problems of waste removal from houses, did not cope with the eventual draining away of their contents. As cities grew – especially London – cesspits overflowed and rivers became extremely polluted and smelly. After the 'Big Stink' in London in 1858, several schemes were considered for draining sewage away from the capital. An engineer called Joseph Bazalgette, devised a scheme based on gravity, whereby the sewage flowed to a chosen outlet on the banks of the Thames at Crossness. Of course, this only led to the shifting of the problem downstream, and eventually, after 1878, a purification works was established there. From the 1870s onwards external soil pipes, made of cast iron, were installed on town houses.

The invention of the earth closet in 1860 helped alleviate a lot of the problems in rural areas, where it was most used. The earth closet, in its simplest form, consisted of a seat with a hole in it and a bucket underneath. Dried, sieved earth was put in the bucket after the closet had been used. The earth was fed into the bucket by means of a lever operating a hopper which was filled with the earth. The bucket was emptied at regular intervals and the contents taken away in a special cart for distribution in suitable rural areas. These earth closets were housed in little shed-like buildings and sited away from the house.

Earth closet

This little model of an earth closet, shown in Fig 11.1, was made to 1/12 scale. It measures 3in (76mm) wide, 2¾in (70mm) deep, and slopes from 7½in (190mm) at the back to 6½in (165mm) at the front.

Materials
Obeche wood
Paint: brown, red, and black
Corrugated cardboard
Miniature door handle

Method
1   Cut the sides and back from the obeche wood, and score each to look like planks.
2   Paint each piece on the outside only.
3   Cut a piece from the corrugated cardboard for the roof, and paint it to resemble weathered corrugated iron.
4   Construct the shed, using strips of wood to form a framework.
5   Make a door from the obeche wood, scoring each side to look like planks. Stick three horizontal planks across the inside. Paint the outside of the door and attach with hinges to open out.
6   Fix a door handle to the outside.
7   Stick pieces of wood to the back of the shed for the hopper (in which the dried earth was placed), and paint it black.
8   Make the seat from plain wood, cutting a hole from the centre. Run a strip of wood across the back, and a reinforcing strip underneath. Leave the seat unpainted; it would have been hygienically scrubbed in real life.

Fig 11.1 Model earth closet in 1/12 scale.

Chapter 12
Obtaining information from buildings

If you see a house which has some details that you would like to use in your dolls' house, you may wish to take some photographs. The main point to remember is not to give the people who live there cause for alarm in thinking that their house is being noted for burglars' information or a road-widening proposal!

Residents who live in well-known beauty spots are more used to their houses being photographed than those in lesser known areas. It is courteous to knock on the door and explain that you would like to use some of their details in your dolls' house. It is best always to travel with a friend, especially in more remote places. You should take photographs from the public footpath – do not try and hide or you will look suspicious. It isn't likely that you will be taking photographs of military or naval establishments, politically important buildings or the homes of celebrities, but do be careful to avoid landing in trouble! This all seems rather alarming, but is only really common sense.

Recording information

Having issued these warnings, we can now think about some practical hints on obtaining measurements from buildings. When photographing, take a direct front view where possible, as well as some from various angles to show such things as the overhang of roofs and the recession of windows, doors, and porches.

Dimensions

If the building is brick, count the courses of bricks in the whole building, the courses taking up the height of windows and doors, and those occupying the space between openings. To make your calculations from fairly regular brickwork, take the depth of a brick and its joint as 3in (76mm), and the length of a brick and its joint as 9in (229mm).

If the house is built of any material other than regular bricks, it is more difficult to assess measurements. Look at the front door itself, excluding the frame or any decorative surround, and consider its height in relation to the average human figure – say 5ft 6in (168cm). If possible, have a friend stand in front of it. Compare your friend's height – you can measure it later – with the height of the door. An average height might be the same as an old cottage door, but a Georgian door might show one and a quarter times the average human height – about 7ft (213cm).

Having assessed the height of the door, relate the proportion of openings and solid spaces to it. Also, see how many times the height of the door will go into the height of the building, if you require this dimension.

If it is possible to see the end of the building, note the pitch of the roof relative to its walls. If this is not possible, note the roofing material itself and, later, use the recommended pitch for it.

Measurements

It is useful to carry a dressmaker's tape measure. (Of course, if you have planned with the owner to make a more careful survey, you will have more sophisticated equipment, but for unplanned work, a tape measure is useful.) If you are on a casual outing and have no measuring devices, but have an umbrella or walking stick, these can be brought into use. Use them for obtaining the heights and lengths you require and note these down in terms of umbrella or stick lengths. You can then measure these when you get home and make the necessary conversions. An architect in the early twentieth century once did a survey of a small building using his umbrella. On his sketch plan he noted various dimensions such as 3B, 4½B, 9B etc. This puzzled his assistant, who was drawing out the plan, until it was explained to him that the letter 'B' stood for Brolly, which was short for umbrella, but the assistant still had to know the length of the umbrella to complete his task!

Principal movements influencing architecture

Gothic and Gothic revival

Gothic is a term used to describe the mediaeval architecture of Western Europe from the thirteenth to the fifteenth centuries. The Gothic revival style of the nineteenth century was based, architecturally, on the designs of that time. The style was characterized by the construction of steep roofs and gables, circular turrets, deep porches, pointed arches, carved woodwork, imitation Tudor half-timber construction, and a general feeling of interesting irregularity.

Classical and classical revival

An interest in travel, first made possible in Georgian times, led aristocrats, scholars, and the moneyed to embark on what was termed 'The Grand Tour'. This tour took in Europe, especially the centres of culture including Greece and Italy. Both of these countries possessed archaelogical remains from the classical age. Italy also possessed buildings from the Renaissance period (which began in Italy in the early part of the fifteenth century), which owed their design to classical influence. Travellers brought back sketches, paintings and artefacts, and cultivated an interest in classical design in England. This interest was taken into the field of architecture and contributed to the development of the Georgian style. There was an intense revival of interest in the classical style during the Victorian period.

The designs of classical revival buildings were based on regularity in plan and symmetry in elevation. Details included detached columns, colonnades and cornices based on the details found in Greek and Roman temples, shallow-pitched roofs, and carefully proportioned sash windows, sometimes with a triangular head called a pediment. They gave a feeling of organized dignity.

Arts and Crafts

The Arts and Crafts movement was started by William Morris with the founding of his firm, Morris and Co., in 1861. Morris and Co. was devoted to the production of craftsman-made furniture, textiles, wallpaper, and stained glass. The movement was characterized by plain, well-produced work, and decorative design elements derived from mediaeval sources. While its influence was felt mainly in the sphere of interior design, a few homes showed an all-round influence, a fine example being the 'Red House', built by Philip Webb for William Morris himself.

Queen Anne revival

The Queen Anne style, as it was generally called, evolved from about 1860, and was widely used from the 1870s onwards. At this time there was a growing interest in, and appreciation of, plain, domestic building based on materials used traditionally, rather than those from industrial mass production. This style was an off-shoot from the Arts and Crafts movement, but used ideas from the Stuart period rather than those from mediaeval times, as William Morris had done.

The Queen Anne style developed and was used in seaside buildings, shops and schools as well as houses. Details included hand-made red bricks, steep clay-tiled roofs, clay tiles hung on walls, little domes and cupolas, dormer windows, and lots of external white-painted woodwork. Seaside houses had painted wooden verandahs, while houses generally had porches with white-painted, turned wooden balusters.

Picturesque

The term Picturesque was used in the eighteenth century to describe garden layouts based on pictures of the Italian masters. Details included artificially constructed Gothic and classical 'ruins', grottos and overgrown pathways. The idea had a tendency to be overdone: ivy-clad ruins, damp grottos, and in one case, a resident hermit, led to a general movement away. However, the Picturesque in terms of building grew out of this idea.

In the eighteenth and early nineteenth centuries, the building of Picturesque cottages became one of the favourite pastimes of the landed gentry. Some cottages were built using local materials and skills, and were arranged in interesting layouts, while in others, the design of the cottages took over from their function, and the strange and quirky results looked more as if they belonged to theatre sets. A favourite detail was to use rustic tree trunks to support a thatched roof, which overhung a pathway in front of the cottage. Ornately carved bargeboards, latticed windows with diamond-shaped panes of glass, walls built of chunky rocks, and cottages built to look like toy castles all found a place.

Bibliography

Billett, **M**, *Thatching and Thatched Buildings*,
Robert Hale Ltd, London, 1979

Brunskill, **R W**, *Illustrated Handbook of Vernacular Architecture*,
Faber and Faber, London, 1970

Clifton-Taylor, **A**, *The Pattern of English Building*,
Faber and Faber, London, 1972

Evans, **T** and **Lycett Green**, **C**, *English Cottages*,
Weidenfeld and Nicolson Ltd, London, 1983

Gould, **R**, *The Complete Victorian House Book*,
Sidgwick and Jackson Ltd, London, 1989

Harris, **R**, *Discovering Timber-Framed Buildings*,
Shire Publications Ltd, Aylesbury, 1986

Jackson, **A** and **Day**, **D**, *Collins Complete Home Restoration Manual*,
HarperCollins Publications, London, 1992

Penoyre, **J** and **J**, *Houses in the Landscape*,
Faber and Faber, London, 1978

Powell, **C**, *Discovering Cottage Architecture*,
Shire Publications Ltd, Aylesbury, 1987

Prizeman, **J**, *Your House: The Outside View*,
Hutchinson Books Ltd, London, 1975

Woodforde, **J**, *Georgian Houses for All*,
Routledge & Kegan Paul, London, 1978

Metric conversion table

Inches to millimetres and centimetres

MM – millimetres   CM – centimetres

Inches	MM	CM	Inches	CM	Inches	CM
⅛	3	0.3	9	22.9	30	76.2
¼	6	0.6	10	25.4	31	78.7
⅜	10	1.0	11	27.9	32	81.3
½	13	1.3	12	30.5	33	83.8
⅝	16	1.6	13	33.0	34	86.4
¾	19	1.9	14	35.6	35	88.9
⅞	22	2.2	15	38.1	36	91.4
1	25	2.5	16	40.6	37	94.0
1¼	32	3.2	17	43.2	38	96.5
1½	38	3.8	18	45.7	39	99.1
1¾	44	4.4	19	48.3	40	101.6
2	51	5.1	20	50.8	41	104.1
2½	64	6.4	21	53.3	42	106.7
3	76	7.6	22	55.9	43	109.2
3½	89	8.9	23	58.4	44	111.8
4	102	10.2	24	61.0	45	114.3
4½	114	11.4	25	63.5	46	116.8
5	127	12.7	26	66.0	47	119.4
6	152	15.2	27	68.6	48	121.9
7	178	17.8	28	71.1	49	124.5
8	203	20.3	29	73.7	50	127.0

Index

About the author

J oyce Percival has had a wealth of experience working for councils on various architectural projects since qualifying as an architect in 1950. With the Greater London Council (formerly the LCC) she worked in the Architects Department for 18 years, on new school buildings and on the layout and landscaping of Expanded Towns. Following this she worked for both the Lewisham and Greenwich Councils as Conservation Architect. Over her 12 years in this position, Joyce gave advice on the repair and alteration of historic and architecturally interesting buildings, and worked on environmental improvement schemes.

In 1975, for European Architectural Heritage Year, Joyce worked in conjunction with the Department of the Environment, the Civic Trust and the Historic Buildings section of the Greater London Council on schemes in Blackheath and Greenwich. She was elected a Fellow of the Royal Society of Arts in the same year for her work with people on improving the environment.

In addition to dolls' houses, Joyce's hobbies include drawing, painting, photography and embroidery – before embarking on her architectural training, she spent some time at Blackheath and Tunbridge Wells Schools of Art. Joyce has a long-held interest in the small buildings of Britain and the physical and social conditions which produced them, together with the lifestyle of their occupants, and she now delights in indulging this interest in the building and furnishing of her dolls' houses.

Titles available from GMC Publications

Books

Carving Birds and Beasts **GMC Publications**

Practical tips for Turners & Carvers **GMC Publications**

Useful Woodturning Projects **GMC Publications**

Woodturning Techniques **GMC Publications**

Woodworkers' Career and Educational Source Book
  GMC Publications

Woodworkers' Courses & Source Book
  GMC Publications

Woodworking Crafts Annual **GMC Publications**

Woodworking Plans and Projects **GMC Publications**

40 More Woodworking Plans and Projects
  GMC Publications

Green Woodwork **Mike Abbott**

Easy to Make Dolls' House Accessories **Andrea Barham**

Making Little Boxes from Wood **John Bennett**

Woodturning Masterclass **Tony Boase**

Furniture Restoration and Repair for Beginners
  Kevin Jan Bonner

Woodturning Jewellery **Hilary Bowen**

The Incredible Router **Jeremy Broun**

Electric Woodwork **Jeremy Broun**

Woodcarving: A Complete Course **Ron Butterfield**

Making Fine Furniture: Projects **Tom Darby**

Restoring Rocking Horses **Clive Green & Anthony Dew**

Heraldic Miniature Knights **Peter Greenhill**

Make Your Own Dolls' House Furniture
  Maurice Harper

Practical Crafts: Seat Weaving **Ricky Holdstock**

Multi-centre Woodturning **Ray Hopper**

Complete Woodfinishing **Ian Hosker**

Practical Crafts: Woodfinishing Handbook **Ian Hosker**

Woodturning: A Source Book of Shapes **John Hunnex**

Making Shaker Furniture **Barry Jackson**

Upholstery: A Complete Course **David James**

The Upholsterer's Pocket Reference Book
  David James

Upholstery Techniques and Projects **David James**

Designing and Making Wooden Toys **Terry Kelly**

Making Dolls' House Furniture **Patricia King**

Making Victorian Dolls' House Furniture
  Patricia King

Making and Modifying Woodworking Tools
  Jim Kingshott

The Workshop **Jim Kingshott**

Sharpening: The Complete Guide **Jim Kingshott**

Turning Wooden Toys **Terry Lawrence**

Making Board, Peg and Dice Games
  Jeff & Jennie Loader

Making Wooden Toys and Games
  Jeff & Jennie Loader

Bert Marsh: Woodturner **Bert Marsh**

The Complete Dolls' House Book **Jean Nisbett**

The Secrets of the Dolls' House Makers **Jean Nisbett**

Wildfowl Carving, Volume 1 **Jim Pearce**

Make Money from Woodturning **Ann & Bob Phillips**

Guide to Marketing **Jack Pigden**

The Complete Pyrography **Stephen Poole**

Woodcarving Tools, Materials and Equipment
  Chris Pye

Carving on Turning **Chris Pye**

Making Tudor Dolls' Houses **Derek Rowbottom**

Making Georgian Dolls' Houses **Derek Rowbottom**

Making Period Dolls' House Furniture
  Derek & Sheila Rowbottom

Woodturning: A Foundation Course **Keith Rowley**

Turning Miniatures in Wood **John Sainsbury**

Pleasure and Profit from Woodturning **Reg Sherwin**

Making Unusual Miniatures **Graham Spalding**

Woodturning Wizardry **David Springett**

Adventures in Woodturning **David Springett**

Furniture Projects **Rod Wales**

Decorative Woodcarving **Jeremy Williams**

Videos

Dennis White	Teaches Woodturning
	Part 1 Turning Between Centres
	Part 2 Turning Bowls
	Part 3 Boxes, Goblets and Screw Threads
	Part 4 Novelties and Projects
	Part 5 Classic Profiles
	Part 6 Twists and Advanced Turning
John Jordan	Bowl Turning

John Jordan	Hollow Turning
Jim Kingshott	Sharpening the Professional Way
Jim Kingshott	Sharpening Turning and Carving Tools
Ray Gonzalez	Carving a Figure: The Female Form
David James	The Traditional Upholstery Workshop
	Part I: Drop-in and Pinstuffed Seats
David James	The Traditional Upholstery Workshop
	Part II: Stuffover Upholstery

GMC Publications regularly produces new books and videos on a wide range of woodworking and craft subjects, and an increasing number of specialist magazines, all available on subscription:

Magazines

WOODTURNING   WOODCARVING   BUSINESSMATTERS

All these publications are available through bookshops and newsagents, or may be ordered by post from the publishers at:
166 High Street, Lewes, East Sussex BN7 1XU
Telephone (01273) 477374, Fax (01273) 478606
Credit card orders are accepted

PLEASE WRITE OR PHONE FOR A FREE CATALOGUE